Peaks and Valleys

My Personal Journey and Search for Lifes Meanings

By

Diane M. How

NGOB Publishing
12241 Tilney Court
Woodbridge, VA 22192

ISBN: 0-9674901-7-0

Library of Congress Control Number TXu 1-769-722

Author's Notes

My heart begins to race when I see the familiar incline fast approaching. The flutter in my stomach increases as each foot of blacktop disappears beneath the car. From the deep recesses of my mind, I hear my grandfather's voice warn *it's a tummy-tickler*.

I resist the urge to apply the brake. I know the pavement continues on the other side, but the fear and thrill of cresting the hill is the same every time. For a split second, I hold my breath. The car flies over the top, nearly airborne, and I enjoy the rush as I land safely on the other side.

Like my pleasure ride through the rolling Ozark countryside, life has been a series of **Peaks and Valleys** which have brought laughter and lament along the way, sometimes both at the same time.

These are the tales that cause a smile to spread across my weathered face as I reminisce about a childhood memory or share a funny anecdote from married life. My memoir would not be complete without lingering for a moment on the heartaches that also left my face damp from tears.

The stories have become enhanced or distorted by subconscious emotions and aging brain cells, into recollections all my own. They are true to the best of my knowledge and memory. If a name is not mentioned, it was not meant to slight anyone, for there are many tales left untold, but not forgotten.

Enjoy the ride.

ACKNOWLEDGEMENTS

Many thanks to Lavern (Wart) How, my husband of forty years, for his patience and understanding, to Laura, my daughter, for her continuous support of my ineptness with computers and her editing efforts, and to Rob, my brother, and Carol, my sister, for their interest, insight, critique and encouragement.

I would be remiss if I failed to mention my good friends, Connie Murphree, Gladys O'Banion and Joyce Richard, who have listened, laughed and cried with me as I traveled through the ***Peaks and Valleys***.

The Pen to Paper Writing Club members provided helpful critiques and suggestions along the way. If it hadn't been for our meetings, I wouldn't have met my editor and friend, Amanda Bretz, and her husband, Brandon Bretz, who created the book cover.

This book would never have been published without the time-consuming efforts and encouragement by my dear friend, Jerome Lee Pionk, Ph D, who always finds a way to make others succeed. A tip of the hat to his son, LTC Jerome Lester Pionk, who also provided assistance.

DEDICATION

Life is a series of blessings and challenges. From the day we are born, we are taught by those around us how to respond to experiences we have using the tools we are given. The values and morals my parents taught me have served me well in deciding which roads to travel. The faith and love my grandparents instilled in me provided the confidence to experience the **Peaks and Valleys**. Every lesson they taught me, whether I liked it or not, made me stronger and helped define the person I am today. I wish they were here to thank in person.

Prologue

Pine Lawn was a typical metropolitan community just four miles north of the city limits of St. Louis, Missouri. In the 1950's, doors were never locked and windows were always open, unless it was the heart of winter. Every evening, from blocks away, you could hear a father shout out "Steve and Nicky, time for dinner." That's how kids were called home or visitors announced. A shout from the sidewalk was the preferred method of communication for most.

Our five-room, brick bungalow was on Bircher Avenue, just off Jennings Station Road, and across the street from the Bethesda Lutheran Church. Although the restless motion of children was always present, it was quiet by most standards, considering it was home to two adults and seven children.

Families in the area were well established. Everyone knew their neighbors within two or three blocks by name. Kids were always outside riding their bikes or playing tag. If it was raining, they were sitting on the porch playing Sorry or Clue. Every girl had Barbie dolls and stuffed in every boy's pocket was a Yo-yo.

The milkman would be seen every morning at the same time making his deliveries. The produce man would yell out "Strawberries… watermelons" as he traveled down the street. Life was simple.

My maternal grandparents, Non and Gramps, as they were known to me, were influential in my upbringing and were the source of many of my happiest memories. They lived a block away and owned the house in which we lived.

My grandmother, who was prim and proper, wore her tinted brown hair in a tight perm. She never left the house without applying a touch of red lipstick to her mouth and a smudge of pink rouge to her cheeks. She was almost secretive about her life before she married my grandfather.

The only glimpse of Non's past comes from a cherished picture. She sat askew on a motorcycle, wearing a sassy hat, sleeveless dress and heels. The grandmother I knew was much more serious and, while she could laugh, it was reserved for special occasions. She was always dressed conservatively, wearing cotton dresses or a double knit suit, if going to church. She never started the day without first putting on a pinafore apron.

Gertrude Westerhoff, aka: Non

My grandfather was tall and lanky with silver hair. He retired from the U.S. Postal Service at an early age and spent many hours taking care of his gum ball and charm machines, which were displayed throughout many stores in town. He invested his earnings in real estate and was well known in Pine Lawn as a stern, but fair, business man. He did a great imitation of a grumpy old man; in reality, he was a kindhearted soul who had a passion for life.

Mom was quiet, soft spoken, and unselfish to a fault. Her auburn, shoulder- length hair accentuated her slim, attractive face, though she never knew her own beauty. She glided across a room with graceful prudence, quiet and purposeful. She once told me that the one thing she did right in life was to have lots of children. My mother was completely devoted to my father and stood by his decisions, even when she knew he was wrong.

When I look at my father's military portrait from 1945, it is easy to see how my mother fell in love with him. He could have passed for the late actor, Robert Mitchum,, as he stood tall in his crisply pressed Army Air Corps attire. He faithfully wrote love letters to Mom from Okinawa, Japan, as he served his tour of duty with the 316th Bomber Wing. Upon his return to the states, much to the dismay of my grandmother, he married my mother.

Dad worked hard all his life. When he wasn't putting in long hours as an expediter at Moloney Electric Transformer Company, he was trying to keep a car running. He often was strict and sullen, but there were times when he worked in the rose garden as he kept a watchful eye on the grill so the barbeque chicken wouldn't burn. The Cardinal baseball game could be heard in the background.

PFC Robert A. Hootselle, Army Air Corps

Some Saturday mornings, Dad would open all the windows and croon to his favorite tune with Mitch Miller or Eddy Arnold. He knew every word to every vinyl album in his limited collection. His passion for music resounded in his deep, baritone voice.

My great-grandparents had passed on by the time I was born, but even they left their mark. My great-grandfather had come to St. Louis from Germany and was a devout Roman Catholic. He helped build the first St. Paul the Apostle Catholic Church in Pine Lawn, donating land and building materials. Because of the legacy, my grandparents felt it was inherent that all grandchildren attend St. Paul's school, even though my parents could not afford it. Gramps covered the cost of tuition for most of the grandkids through eighth grade.

Our family may have lived a paltry life in comparison to others, but we always had a roof over our head and food on the table. The tales of struggles taught me humility and great appreciation for simple things in life. The joys help remind me of the importance of family.

Chapter One

Just Trying to Get By

You would think being a kid growing up in fifties would be the easiest part of life. According to my parents, the only things I had to worry about were to do well in school, show up for dinner on time and complete my chores. That sounds simple, but it seemed a lot more complex to me when I was just a kid.

Every morning I would march up the long isle in church to the first pew on the left. Girls in the first grade always sat in the front pew during Mass; boys were on the right. The minute I reached my seat, I would start fretting. For a little kid, it was like playing Simon says without words. I had to watch the priest and remember what to do next. It was so confusing. Was it genuflect, kneel, sit, stand, kneel, or genuflect, stand, kneel, sit? Even if by chance I got it right, I had to do it quickly and without making a sound. That was nearly impossible with those heavy wooden kneelers that weren't made for little hands. When I dropped one, it echoed throughout the whole church and everyone knew I messed up.

I was so nervous I wanted to bite my fingernails, but I had to keep my hands firmly pressed together and pointed to Heaven at all times. I reviewed all the rules in my head. No talking or turning around. Don't forget to bow my head when the priest says Jesus. Do you know how many times the priest said Jesus during one Mass? I felt like one of those dogs that sits in the back of a car window and bobs up and down, but I couldn't think about that or I would laugh.

It wasn't like I could slack off at any time. The nuns not only had eyes in the back of their heads, they also could anticipate if I even thought about resting my behind on the edge of the pew when I was kneeling. They didn't have to say a word. They had the LOOK. It didn't take a mind reader to understand the message. I could feel the look when they were sitting behind me. It made the hairs on my neck stand up.

Once I had all those rules imprinted in my head, it was time to memorize all the prayers and responses for Mass. There are the Lord's Prayer, the Hail Mary, the Apostles' Creed (which is not to be confused with the Nicene Creed), the Act of Contrition, the Rosary, and dozens more. That's like a gazillion things to remember at the age of six. That was not easy.

It didn't get any better when classes started. First, there was math. Every day I practiced addition and subtraction. When I got in trouble, which was inevitable, the punishment was to write my times tables a hundred times for homework. They did that to make sure my parents found out about me being in trouble.

Next, we practiced printing the alphabet. The letters had to be perfect. I loved writing on the special paper with lines on it, but I didn't like when my pencil would break. The only sharpener was in the front of the room. Everyone looked at me and snickered like I had gum stuck to my shoe or something. When I got back to my desk, I would try to remember how to make a lower case *a*, but by then the whole class was working on printing a *b*. Ugh!

The first time I had a nun as a teacher, I was scared to death. There is nothing comforting about a lady dressed in a scary black cloak. She reminded me of the Grim Reaper that scared me one Halloween. The nun walked up and down the rows tapping a long, wooden pointer on the desks, just to intimidate everyone in class. It worked. When I heard the sound of that stick coming, I couldn't remember my name.

When school let out, I would meet up with my two older brothers, Rob, who was three years older than me and Larry who was just a year older. We walked together, but we seldom took a direct route home. Sometimes we stopped to look in the window at   L-D's Dry Goods Store to see if they changed the display. My grandmother would take me there every August to buy me a pair of saddle shoes and a uniform. They were supposed to last all school year, but I guess I was heavy on my feet because by February, my feet got wet every time it snowed.

The printing shop was next door to L-D's. Boxes of poster paints, like the ones we used for finger painting in school, were on display, especially during the month of October. Most businesses would let the older kids in the neighborhood paint a scary picture on their big window. They had a contest at Halloween to see whose picture was the best.

Hilbert's Bakery was across the street and I could smell the delicious baked goods even if we didn't stop in the store. They had the best iced caked donuts in the world. The display cases were all glass so I could look at the cakes and cookies as long as I didn't leave fingerprints.

Scott's Market was along the way, but we didn't go in there very often. The owners weren't too keen on kids being in the store without their parents.

Next, we'd peek in the window at the laundromat to see if anyone was in there. If it was empty, we would go in and search for loose change under the washers and dryers. If a neighbor would see us, they'd call Mom on the party line and she'd be waiting for us at the door when we got home. I think the idea of Neighborhood Watch was born in Pine Lawn.

If we found a nickel under a washer, we'd stop at Gross' Market for some penny candy. I knew the cost of every item at the candy counter. I also tried to learn the price of every other item in the store so I could tell Mom how much it would cost when she wanted us to buy something. Mom never left the house, probably because she always had a baby to watch. My brothers and I did the grocery shopping. We never needed any money because Mr. Gross let us put it on a tab.

My grandparents shopped at Scotts' Market. I always thought it was strange that they didn't shop at the same place as we did since it was closer to their house. As I got older, I suspected it was because of the bill that was usually over due. One time, my brother had to ask my grandfather to help us because we couldn't put any more on the tab until it was paid.

Rules didn't stop when school was over. In fact, they were mild compared to the discipline enforced at home. No slamming doors; no running inside, no friends in the house, no sassing back, answer "yes, sir" or "no, sir," don't ask questions and don't tell anyone anything. Those were the reasonable ones. My father had a few more that made it easy to have an infraction at any moment of the day. There was no talking allowed while doing the dishes, homework or at bedtime. This was tough for a chatter box like me. Oh, and no snacks between meals and no getting out of bed at night.

Once we got in bed, if there was any noise, no matter how slight or what the source, punishment was a belt whipping for each one of us. We would have to sit on the edge of the bed and wait our turn. The waiting was the worst part of the punishment for me.

Mom was expected to enforce the rules when Dad was at work, although one of her favorite sayings was "Just wait until your father comes home!" One afternoon, Mom came into the kitchen and caught my little sister with a slice of bologna in her hand. I watched as Mom's hand landed firmly on Carol's tiny butt. The lunchmeat flew out of her hand and stuck firmly to the ceiling. It was hilarious. Of course, I received a spanking, too, for laughing, but I couldn't help it. I could still see the circle left from that piece of bologna years later, even though it had been painted many times.

Another time, Carol and I were sitting at the table. I was doing my homework. While we weren't allowed to talk, that didn't keep us from making funny faces when we thought Mom wasn't watching. Carol tried to suppress a laugh and it came out something like a quack. In a very stern voice, Mom said "Was that you, Carol?"

"No, it was a duck," my sister blurted out. Once again, laughter prevailed. We both got spanked. I always wondered how my mother kept from laughing too.

Much to my dismay, my response to any punishment or harsh words from my father was to cry. This only made things worse. He saw tears as weakness and he wanted us kids to be tough. I was anything, but tough. No matter how hard I tried, I couldn't make the tears stop once they started, so I tended to do whatever was necessary to avoid getting in trouble.

One time, I was sure God intervened on my behalf. Carol and I slept in a double bed right next to my parents' room. The bed frame was not very dependable. It had two pieces of wood which were balanced across the frame to hold the box spring in place. If the slats were centered perfectly and no one moved, it might hold until morning.

We were sound asleep when I was jolted awake with a loud thump. My head was nearly on the ground and my feet up in the air. The slat on my side of the bed had fallen. My heart was pounding, but I held my breath hoping Dad did not hear the noise. I laid there motionless for what seemed like hours. By some miracle, Dad didn't come in. He didn't even yell. I stayed in the same position until morning, even though my head hurt from the blood rushing to it all night.

I was an optimist even as a child. I tried hard to make good grades and stay out of trouble, hoping it would warrant a pat on the back or an "Atta girl." Those kinds of things didn't happen in our house, but I kept trying.

I almost felt Dad recognized my efforts once when he yelled at Rob and Larry, "Why can't you be more like Diane."

Any chance of his words having a positive effect on my self esteem evaporated with the anger my brothers showed toward me afterwards. As hard as it was for me growing up, my brothers had it tougher because they were always in trouble.

Chapter Two

Parents versus Grandparents

My grandparents had lots of free time so they came by nearly every morning for a cup of tea or coffee. Just before they arrived, Mom would start fussing at us to get the rooms cleaned up. Come to think of it, there was always a cold tension in the air, like when you had to go to the principal's office.

My family did not believe in showing affection with lots of hugs and kisses. In fact, I can't remember a time when my grandparents embraced Mom or told her they loved her, even though she was their only child and she was so dutiful to them.

Fortunately for us grandkids, we got a squeeze now and then and lots of smiles, at least most of the time. We visited them almost daily after school. Gramps would spend hours with my brothers, Rob and Larry, in the basement or outside teaching them those things they would need to know as they grew into men. They mowed grass, changed oil in the car, and built bird houses using all the hand tools on the workbench.

My grandmother taught me things I would need to know when I got married. According to Non, a woman's role was to take care of the man of the house, raise children and entertain company. I pushed the sweeper, washed windows, and learned to measure sugar and flour while making cookies and cakes. A pot of stew or soup was always brewing on the stove and made the room smell wonderful.

Mom, Dad, Rob, Larry, Carol and Diane

There were little things that they did to make us feel special. If one of us was home sick with a cold, my grandparents would deliver a can of tomato juice, a box of tea bags, and some tissues to comfort us. If it was raining, Gramps would be waiting outside of school with his car to give us a ride home. They disciplined us with a gentler voice and rewarded us with praise on occasion.

After Mass on Sunday morning, I couldn't wait to get home, change my clothes and skip merrily down the block to my grandparents' house. Their brick home, smartly trimmed in white, prominently faced Jennings Road at the corner of Westerhoff, a street named after my grandfather's family. It's was on a large, double lot, perfect for playing tag or running through the sprinkler on a hot summer day.

Two massive pine trees provided a formal, yet inviting introduction to the right corner of the lot. Its branches were just high enough to allow young kids to sneak underneath it, where they might sip a cold pop or eat some penny candy before dinner. Often the proof was left behind and one of us grandkids would be sent into the hidden cove to retrieve the trash.

The front porch had two sturdy, metal chairs where my grandparents would sit in the evenings and wave to the neighbors. Two concrete flower pots always spilled over with red Geraniums and Zinnias.

If the wooden front door was opened, it was an invitation for anyone to announce their arrival, pull open the screen door and come in. If the front door was closed, that meant it was nap time and I shouldn't disturb them.

The green, short-napped carpet in the living room matched the two armchairs that sat on either side of the hi-fi stereo. An elegant lamp sat on each of the corner tables and provided just enough light in the room for reading the paper. It was angled to the side so there was enough room for a coffee cup and handkerchief. Non always had a handkerchief close at hand in case she needed to clean the dirt off my face.

Gramps would have a glass of wine or bottle of beer on his table. He started each day with a sip of wine. Then, at eleven a.m., not a minute before, you could hear the cap pop off a bottle of beer. I seldom saw him drink more than two, unless they had company.

There was enough room on the living room floor to spread three blankets and pillows out without spilling over into the dining room. On occasion, my brothers and I were invited to sleep over. It was always great fun.

A metal folding table, positioned by my grandfather's arm chair, meant Gramps was ready to beat someone at checkers. Rob and Larry could win sometimes, but not often. On occasion, the dining room table would be filled with gumball machines that needed filling. I loved to help put the tiny charms in plastic capsules for the vending machines. Chiclets, jaw breakers and gum were used to fill some of the other machines.

Gramps was always laughing and teasing. His sense of humor was a little ornery. He kept a metal fly swatter close at hand. If one of us kids walked by, he would sting us on the back of the leg with it. He also liked to pretend to check the thickness of a pants leg as he pinched a little and asked "How thick are those trousers?" He had a hearty laugh that was contagious. I don't ever remember being upset with him for the teasing, but I have to admit, it made me flinch a little every time I went by him.

Before dinner, I helped spread the crisply ironed, white linen cloth over the Formica dining room table. My grandmother instructed me on proper etiquette as I smoothed out any wrinkles. According to Non, every female was expected to know the correct placement of the silverware, glasses and fine china for when they got married.

The table wasn't finished until I carefully opened the glass door of the six-foot tall, cherry wood china cabinet and retrieved two short crystal glasses. I would place one on each end of the table. My grandfather filled them half-way with Mogen David wine for him and my grandmother. The table looked as if someone important was coming to dine, but it was just us kids.

The savory smell of chicken and dressing drifted in from the kitchen and always caused my stomach to growl. Gramps and I would snack on a piece of celery while waiting for the feast to be spread. It became a tradition I still remember each time I take a stalk of celery from the fridge.

All the food had to be on the table and everyone needed to be sitting before we could bless the food and start eating. The skin on the baked chicken was golden and the celery and onion dressing was perfectly browned. The egg noodles had a dusting of bread crumbs on top. The condensed milk made the mashed potatoes creamy and the gravy had a few lumps from the dressing that was left in the bottom of the pan. The steam from the fresh green beans rose to the ceiling. It was a feast fit for a king or queen.

Afterwards, Non and I would clear the table and do the dishes. Rob and Larry would run down the street to visit their friends and Gramps would retire to the bedroom for a short nap.

Non, Gramps, Diane, Rob, Larry and Carol

Sundays were relaxing and enjoyable for the grandkids. Mom and Dad probably enjoyed having some time without us under foot.

My grandparents always made me feel loved and special. I'm pretty sure my parents didn't feel the same way.

Chapter Three

Escaping

Even as a child, I had a need to have a special place in which to escape the stresses of daily life. I loved to sit on our front porch and watch the cars go by and listen to the birds chirp. In the fall, I would rake leaves just so I could look at all the beautiful colors and pretend I was in the country.

In the summer, some kids went to camp or took vacations with their parents. We never had the money for a vacation, but I was really fortunate that my grandparents provided me with an opportunity to get to know what it was like to live outside the city.

Long before interstate highways populated the US, before cars had affordable automatic transmissions, and when a gallon of gasoline cost less than 25 cents, my grandparents found that special place where they could leave their worries behind, and enjoy the peaceful sounds of nature.

The clubhouse near Lawrenceton, Missouri

Lawrenceton, Missouri, was a sleepy little town some sixty or seventy miles from St. Louis in the heart of the Ozarks. I delighted whenever I heard the words, "Pack your clothes; we're going to the country."

Like many families in the 1950's, my aunts and uncles enjoyed filling the weekends with family gatherings and simple pleasures. One of my relatives, Oscar Meyers, bought about twenty-five acres of land where friends and relatives gathered for a few beers, a dip in the creek and bonfires under starlit skies.

There were no telephones or televisions, only the bare essentials when it came to necessities. A meal was simply prepared on a portable grill and served on paper plates.

A swim in the creek served as a bath until Saturday, when a cool shower in the pump house was a must. If the spiders and crickets that shared the space didn't scare me, someone would always be around to throw a handful of rocks on the tin roof just to make me jump.

One of the buildings on the property started out as an old chicken coop. My grandparents added on a screened-in porch, spruced it up and began making memories. The front porch overlooked a lovely valley. The view was breathtaking. A worn, but sturdy, table and a few chairs provided the perfect place to eat our meals.

The rest of the house was just one room that served multiple purposes. It had a weathered sofa sleeper and a rollaway bed that folded up and was stowed in the corner until needed. There was a red table with metal legs, a propane gas stove, a sink with cold running water, and a dependable Philco refrigerator. We boiled water from the pump to wash dishes. An outhouse was just up the hill and it had a crescent moon carved in the door.

One of the other clubhouse structures had enough rooms to house seven or eight families, and was referred to as the "big club." It towered high in the air on sturdy wooden supports. Beneath it hung an old wooden porch swing, my most favorite spot in the world. The bench was worn smooth from years of use and it faced the rugged, steep driveway and miles of tree-filled hillsides.

There was enough room between the big club and Uncle Jack's ranch-style house to have a Wiffle ball game. Trees served as bases and broomsticks as bats. It didn't matter who won as long as every kid had a chance to play. If we couldn't find a Wiffle ball, bottle caps were substituted. The adults who weren't in the game would gather on the patio next to Jack's place to sip on a cold beer and shoot the breeze.

Every spring, summer and fall, my two older brothers and I would help my grandparents load up their 1959 Ford Fairlane, with enough food and water to last a week. Carol, my sister who was four years younger than me, came along when she was old enough to wander around on her own. With great anticipation, we would say goodbye to Mom (Dad was already at work) and begin our trek through the city to Highway 61/67.

It was a slow, long journey, at least for a child who was eager to beat a path to her favorite swing, but I would never complain, even when it was scorching hot in the car. The reward at the end of the trip was worth it all.

We couldn't have the windows down too low or it would blow my grandmother's new perm, but that was understood and we all knew it wasn't up for discussion.

There were two required stops along the way. The first was a produce stand in Festus. It was exciting to see so much fresh food in one place. Non would pick out the most perfect red tomatoes, fresh green beans, and corn-on-the-cob. Gramps would find the biggest homegrown watermelon. With the trunk already full, all of their purchases would be stored by my feet for the rest of the journey.

The second stop was a small roadside park that offered picnic tables and shade under towering cottonwoods. It was often filled with other travelers seeking relief for overheated cars that had steam rising from the engines. We'd savor a special treat of delicious iced cake donuts purchased in advance at Hilbert's Bakery. Fresh milk would be retrieved from the green Coleman cooler and my grandmother would carefully pour it into the collapsible metal cups that were stored in the glove compartment of the car. I marveled at the ingenious invention and was delighted any time we had the chance to use them.

The captivating smell of coffee filled the air when the lid was removed from the heavy metal thermos. Soon, we would have our fill and climb back into the Fairlane, men in front and women in back, oblivious to the sweltering heat of the day. Nothing seemed to matter except getting to the club.

The car hummed efficiently down the hot black top as I eagerly watched for the Dew Drop Inn sign in Bloomsdale. I knew once we turned there, it would be about twenty more minutes to get to our destination.

Rolling hills stirred butterflies in my stomach as my grandfather nudged the gas just at the right moment to evoke a shrill squeal from my throat. The watermelon bumped at my feet as we hugged each turn a little too fast. I knew he did it just to get a rise out of me. My excitement increased as each hill and turn was completed.

We'd pass the disappearing house, a home that would fade out of sight as we drove by it. Then there was Mr. Karen's place where cows, pigs and chickens wandered about the many acres, and the Ponderosa, a well manicured setting with a house positioned among the trees just where I would want it if I was planning to build a place.

Shortly after we passed the little church in Lawrenceton, we turned left at the split in the road and headed toward the low water bridge. It was then that I could see it! The make-shift club house looked like a mansion to me as it towered high on the hill overlooking the corn field.

My excitement was always tempered by the thought of the last half-mile. Gramps would slow down to a crawl for a quick look at the creek as we crossed over the bridge. I could already imagine how good it would feel to jump into the cool, inviting water. Yet, I knew the journey was not done until we conquered the insurmountable hill ahead of us. With my fists clenched and teeth biting my lower lip, we would make our ascent up the endless chalk-white mountain. The clouds of dust in our trail made it impossible to see anything behind us. Once we reached the entrance to the club, we would slow to a stop to make the final lunge up the primitive driveway.

Slabs of rock had been laid by hand to form the crudely graded entrance. My brothers, Rob and Larry, would get out and move any boulders that had fallen in the way. They would then rearrange the flat stones as best as they could and run up the rest of the hill to watch us make the ascent. Gramps would shout out to me and my grandma, "Don't drag your feet!" I don't know if he said that to increase my anxiety, but he was ornery like that. Either way, that's when I would hold my breath and pray.

I knew Gramps had to focus all his efforts on giving it the right amount of gas and releasing the clutch at the right moment without killing the engine. I shivered with fear just worrying about the engine dying and the car rolling backwards into the woods across the road. Somehow, we always made it, but I never stopped feeling anxious until the car was on flat ground and the rocks were placed behind each wheel to keep it from rolling while out of gear. A sense of triumph and relief always was accompanied by a round of sighs from me and my grandma upon completing the challenge.

Within the hour, the car was unloaded, the pump and electric turned on and the dusty old cabin was turned into home. Floors were swept, tables wiped down, and occasionally, a snake had to be removed from his nesting place in the fridge or a dead mouse removed from the folded up rollaway bed. Those things never seemed to detract from the feeling of peace and happiness that we all shared upon arrival at our favorite escape.

The hum of the lawn mower filled the air as my brothers helped Gramps clean up outdoors after Mother Nature had her way while we were gone. Soon, we were free from chores, free from worry; free to roam anywhere within the sound of a voice calling us for dinner; free to swing until my heart was content.

Rob and Larry stayed busy doing "boy" things like shooting their BB guns or taking turns riding the home-made go cart down the hill from hell. The only problem was that if they survived navigating the hill to the bottom, they had to pull the cart all the way back up the hill before the other brother could ride. I really didn't mind not getting a turn.

Other times, they would ride the zip line that was strung between two trees. There were two problems with that adventure. Some of the pieces of wood nailed to the tree for use as a ladder would be missing. If they succeeded in getting to the platform, they would grab the handles, jump off and hang on for dear life. They held out their feet to keep from hitting the tree, of course, they had to still be facing the tree at the end of the run. There were lots of bruises when it didn't work out just right.

Being a girl, this was another fun activity that was out of my league, but I didn't mind missing out on the experience. For me, the best part of being at the club was swinging, singing and thinking.

Now, I had the swinging down pat and plenty of things to think about. I never was good at the singing part, so it helped that I was usually alone while I was listening to my transistor radio. Once, when I was in first grade, Mother Superior was coming to visit our class. I was asked to just move my lips. That pretty much ended my music career, but it never kept me from singing when I was alone.

For the first few minutes when I would settle into the swing, my mind would tend to replay the many lectures my father gave me on all of my many shortcomings.

"Who do you think you are interrupting me when I'm talking? Haven't I told you before not to do that? Didn't I teach you to have respect? Who do you think you are?"

His words echoed again and again. They were always rhetorical questions that demanded no reply. I was just trying to warn him that the hot dogs were burning. I didn't mean to make him mad. The reason never mattered, only following the rules.

My heart ached to please him and it made me sad to be such a disappointment to him. The tears would begin to stream down my cheeks and I would vow to do better when I got back home. I was too young to realize I had no control over anyone else's happiness except my own.

The sound of water splashing over the slab rocks in the creek across the road had a way of washing away my sadness. The lofty white clouds in the sky would mesmerize me and I would let my imagination take me to faraway places. Sometimes I'd close my eyes and inhale deeply to see if I could identify all the smells around me. The scent of freshly mowed hay and the earthy fragrance of a nearby cedar tree would fill my head and I'd rejoice in being back in the arms of my faithful friend.

With one foot on the ground and the other tucked under me on the bench, I could rock to and fro for hours, appreciating every moment.

Just before dusk, Non would call us to dinner and I'd run down the hill kicking up dust in my trail. Gramps would turn the dial on the old radio until he heard the voice of Jack Buck or Harry Cary calling the Cardinal baseball game. By the time dishes were done, a harvest moon and a million stars would fill the sky at night. We'd count lightening bugs as we looked out over the valley. Life was good.

An occasional pair of headlights could be seen from miles away approaching the area, but the car seldom turned down the gravel road in our direction. I didn't mind; the solitude was enjoyable. All of my senses were more acute as I listened for a lizard to scurry across the steps, or try to guess what the neighbors had for dinner from the aroma that drifted over the hill.

My grandma and I would prepare the stowaway bed after dinner dishes were done. A fresh sheet and blanket would be spread out on it and the scent of cedar would wharf in through the small window from a nearby tree. The men put up wooden cots on the porch. Canvas cloths, that had been rolled up and secured at the top of the screened-in porch during the daylight hours, would be dropped so that they would not get damp at night when the fog rolled in. I delighted in listening to my brothers talk with Gramps until I fell asleep. The locust and whippoorwills would sing to me as I drifted off and the cardinal's chirp would greet me at dawn.

When Carol came along, I would sleep on a cot on the porch, which was great because there were no walls to obscure the view of the sky. I could watch for shooting stars before I fell into a deep slumber.

We usually arrived at the club a day or two before everyone else. While I enjoyed the solitude and having the swing all to myself, by Friday, I was ready for company. We would pay special attention to approaching cars, anxious to hear them turn onto the gravel road, hoping it would be carrying aunts, uncles and cousins whom we hadn't seen in months.

Rob and Larry would climb up and sit on top of the stone pillars that marked the entrance to the rugged driveway and watch the stars fill the sky as the moon raised high above the trees.

A few carloads of relatives would arrive before I went to bed, but by morning, cars would be parked throughout any flat opening in the woods and the clubhouses would be overflowing with the hum of chatter. Soon, everyone would be up and about talking about the ride down or sharing something to laugh about. There was plenty of teasing, good cheer, and happiness.

Around noon, everyone changed into swimsuits and grabbed their towels to head to the swimming hole. The older teens would jump in my cousin Terri's red convertible and head to Establishment Creek. The younger cousins would start begging our uncle Jack for a "putt-putt" ride. Soon, he would throw all the inner tubes into the back of his old pickup; the smaller kids and some of the aunts would climb on board, too. They would head for the swimming hole.

Most of the time, my brothers would walk down the dusty hill with my grandfather. Gramps would wear his swimming trunks, a pair of old shoes that were splattered with paint, and a smile on his face. With a towel thrown over his pale broad shoulders, they would take off down the hill.

My grandmother always waited another five minutes before we could leave. She was mortified that Gramps would let anyone see his long, white legs and bare chest. She'd mutter under her breath, but she wouldn't fuss at him because she knew that he was a kid at heart.

Non never changed into a swim suit. She had no intention of getting wet. I watched as she applied her rouge, added a touch of lipstick and made sure every curl was in place before we started walking to the creek. I teased her once about looking good for the cows, but she didn't have much of a sense of humor when it came to her appearance.

Food was always a special treat when we were at the club. My grandfather could fix the best burgers in the world on his small portable grill. One time, he dropped them all in the dirt, but we just dusted them off and ate them anyway. There's just something about fresh country air and the taste of food.

Nothing compared to the smoked jowl and pancakes on Sunday morning after our trip to town for church. The priest alternated between Saint Anne Catholic Church in French Village and Saint Lawrence in Lawrenceton, so we always had to check the schedule ahead of time to be sure what time Mass was being held. Both churches were quaint and beautifully adorned with fresh cut flowers all summer long. The congregation was relaxed and happy to welcome visitors. No one left the service early and everyone stayed afterwards to catch up on the latest gossip.

By Sunday evening, most of the clan had packed their gear and returned to the city. We always stayed an extra day or two to enjoy the peaceful setting. We might take a drive to see our friends, the Grogan's, in nearby Weingarten. It didn't matter to me if we did anything, but just sit. I knew I would finally get a chance to be alone again with my old friend and swing till my heart was content.

I doubt anyone else had the same appreciation for the rugged old swing as I did. That seemed evident when I returned some years later and found it had been taken down when the structural supports that had aged beyond repair were replaced. I miss my old friend, but I will never forget the feeling of peace whenever I was snuggled in its warm embrace.

My Old Friend

You were my friend, you beckoned me
You listened to my pain
You caught my tears, you dried them up
You were my shelter in the rain

Not even once did you turn away
Nor secret did you tell
You listened to my tender thoughts
You knew me oh, so well

The thought of you would comfort me
When we were far away
I'd close my eyes and you'd be there
In your arms I longed to stay

Too young to know our time would end
We'd part our ways too soon
Now cherished memories are all I have
Beneath the harvest moon.

By Diane M. How

Chapter Four

Ready or Not

I was only four years old when Carol was born in 1955. I loved to watch Mom sterilize the bottles and mix the formula. I observed studiously as she changed her diaper while she lay in the tiny bassinette, knowing one day I would be asked to do it. I delighted in getting wet when she would splash merrily in the sink as she was bathed. Her light brown hair fell in ringlets on her slender face.

As Carol grew bigger, I was allowed to help feed her, I held the bottle so she could see it, but not reach it. Her eyes widened with excitement, arms and legs flinging about wildly, as she anticipated the nipple reaching her lips. It was exciting having a newborn in the house.

By the time my two brothers arrived, Keith in 1960 and Craig in 1962, I was old enough to master changing diapers, sterilizing bottles, feeding and bathing. Although I enjoyed playing the role of mommy on occasion, I was not prepared to take on the duties of a nanny full time. My skills would be put to the test much sooner than I anticipated.

Keith Hootselle

Keith was a well-behaved four-year-old with a winning smile that would light up any room when he was in it. He had golden blonde hair and bright blue eyes. On Mother's Day, 1964, Keith complained to Mom that he had "a headache in his stomach." Normally, any tummy problems were treated with a dose of Paregoric. A trip to the doctor was a rare occasion for anyone in our family, since there was no health insurance and money was so tight, still, something told my parents it was necessary.

The morning after the doctor's visit, Mom kept me home from school. It was unusual to skip school and when Mom told me we would be taking the bus, I was even more surprised. At first, I was excited and wanted to know where we were going.

"Keith is sick. I need you to help with Craig." The look on her face told me not to ask any other questions. My excitement began to wane.

As we got onto the bus, I picked out a seat big enough for the four of us. My Grandmother had taken me on the bus to Wellston a few times, so I tried to impress my brothers by pointing out the skating rink and big water tower along the route as we made our way down Natural Bridge. Craig was only two and looked at me wide eyed as if he was impressed. Keith looked like he felt too bad to care. Mom just stared out the window.

It didn't take long to learn this wasn't going to be a fun trip. We were headed to St. Louis Children's Hospital. Mom was silent all throughout the journey. She tried hard to not show it, but her eyes showed fear. Week after week we made the trip. Her face never changed.

As much as I came to dislike the trips to the hospital, because of the toll it took on Keith and Mom, I dreaded Saturdays even more. With the break of dawn, Mom would sit with Keith at the kitchen table. In front of him would be a bowl of applesauce. With each spoon full, he would be given a large white pill to swallow. He struggled to keep them down. If he was unsuccessful, he had to start all over. Each week, the number of pills increased.

After the pills were consumed, the family would load up in our Plymouth station wagon and travel to a medical building in Clayton, where Rob, Larry, Carol, Craig and I stayed in the car. An hour or two later, they returned. There was never any discussion about what they did inside, but somehow I knew it wasn't good.

There was no relief from the routine over the next seven months. Keith got weaker each week. He never complained. I don't remember him crying or throwing a tantrum. He just did what he was told and tried to smile as often as he could. I was amazed at his behavior.

Mom and Dad were stoical. No tears were shed in our presence. Did they wait until we were all asleep to let them fall? If they were angry or sad, they kept it to themselves. Nothing was said to prepare me for the horrible ending.

On New Year's Day, 1965, Dad drove the car as Keith lay helplessly in my mother's arms on the way to the hospital. He said "tell everyone goodbye" and succumbed to the grapefruit-size tumor that grew relentlessly in his stomach.

I felt confused, sad and a little angry that I didn't know he was going to die. I remember that St. Paul the Apostle Church seemed disproportionately large the day of the funeral. The tiny white casket was rolled up the marble floor to the communion rail where it was draped in a white cloth that had a red cross embroidered in the center. Tears streamed down my cheeks, but I looked straight ahead so my father didn't see. The organ music made me feel sadder and I fought off the sobs that welled up in my throat.

The silence that followed in the days after the funeral was unbearable. It was as if we were expected to erase all memory of Keith from our minds. His name was not spoken. His toys and picture were put away into a closet. Dad went to work. Mom went back to her routine of getting us off to school, cooking, cleaning and caring for Craig. There was no emotion, no discussion of the sorrow and loss we experienced together. I didn't understand any of it.

I wondered what it meant to die and what happened to you after the casket was placed in the ground, but I didn't dare ask. The house was quieter than ever and void of any joy. There was no laughing or joking for any reason, at any time. Even my grandparents found it too painful to come around.

Everyone walked around the elephant in the room. Meals were eaten in silence. No matter how much I tried to do the right thing, it was never enough for my father. If the laundry was washed, hung out to dry and folded in neat stacks before Dad came home, he would complain that I should have put everything away.

Dad turned to a brown bottle, unable to deal with his pain. When drunk, he lectured for hours on end. His words were angry and hurtful. His belt whippings were more forceful and frequent. There were times when he used his fists on my brothers. He shoved Larry down the basement stairs and broke numerous ribs.

Mom said nothing, whether it was because she feared my father or felt sorry for him, I never knew. There was no discussion of medical treatment, no apologies. As we had all been trained, no one told of the abuse. Larry moved out.

Life as I had known it was changed and would never be the same again. I prayed with all my heart that God would spare us from death anytime soon.

Chapter Five

Thirteen and Working

I wanted to do anything I could to ease the stress in our house. Since money was always an issue, I decided it was time to find a job. Ollie Gross, who owned the market where we shopped, gave me my first job in the spring of 1965. My brothers had worked there, so it seemed a natural transition for me to follow in their footsteps.

I stocked shelves, cleaned floors and windows, and helped at the meat counter whenever they got busy. My starting pay was fifty cents an hour. Lucille, Ollie's wife, watched me carefully. Within a few months, I was taught to run the cash register and was given a raise. I felt a sense of pride and saw an opportunity to pay Ollie back for hiring me.

Instead of taking the extra pay, I asked him to keep track of how much money I earned and apply it to the bill we owed. On Christmas day, I presented my parents with a receipt showing $75.00 had been paid off the balance of the bill. A tear fell from Mom's eyes. Dad just looked at me and didn't say anything. Somehow, I think it made him feel worse. He was a proud man and it was difficult for him to accept help from his daughter.

In the fall of 1965, I attended Normandy Senior High School. It was a great distraction from the darkness that loomed within our house. It didn't take long to see the differences between public and private school. I felt lost in the unfamiliar environment. There were multiple large buildings to negotiate between, rather than one small one. I had many nightmares in which I reported to the wrong class at the wrong time in the wrong place. Just finding my locker was a challenge.

It was difficult to go from a "don't speak unless spoken to" environment to a place where there were ten times as many students, all talking at once. My lack of self confidence and social skills did nothing to help the situation. I was the typical wall flower through most of my high school years.

My comfort zone seemed to be in English Composition. As long as we were focusing on diagramming a sentence or composing a thought on paper, I was happy. Oral communications was a different story. If I had to give a report in front of class, I resembled a bowl of gelatin. My legs and voice competed in a quivering contest. Even if I could squeak out a sound, no one could hear me. I was ready to break into tears at the slightest urging.

My relationship with my brothers had changed over the years. They no longer competed with me for attention from Mom and Dad. My oldest brother, Rob, was driving by then. On a few occasions, we would skip Mass on Sunday and go to the Riverview Circle in Baden for a burger. He called it "Steak 'n Shake Mass." I always feared we would get caught, but I went without complaining. I was proud to be cruising where popular kids hung out.

Mom delivered Michelle on October 12, 1967 at the age of forty. Her birth brought joy to a house where it was most needed. Unfortunately, Rob had to deliver some bad news to dad that same day. He had a wreck on Lucas and Hunt Road and totaled the '65 Chevy, Impala that he had just purchased. He was not hurt, at least not before he told my father. I remember it was my grandparent's anniversary too. Talk about a mixed bag of emotions.

I also worked at K Studio, an imprinted product company, where the owner was quite taken with the Batman mania that was sweeping the country. He was thrilled when he received orders for thousands of the T-shirts. The employees, my cousin and I, had to remove each shirt from the box, shake it to remove the cardboard that was stuck inside of it, slip it onto the conveyor belt, and smooth it out to remove any folds or creases in the fabric. The machine held about three dozen shirts, so I had to be quick about it.

Mr. K would place the paint screen on each shirt and apply the Batman design. The shirts would travel another few feet before passing underneath where heating elements dried the paint quickly. As it came back around, we would remove the shirt, fold it, and place it neatly in a box. There were no windows and no air condition in the huge warehouse.

I didn't mind the heat or the hard work, but as each shirt passed, my boss would mimic the characters in the movie by yelling "Wham! Pow! Zam!," over and over again. Maybe the 115 degrees tempered my humor, but I could have strangled him by the time we shut down the machines at the end of each day.

Chapter Six

Love and Marriage

It was about 1970 when I met my future husband, Wart. I had seen him occasionally at Gross Market, but I didn't think he had noticed me. He was born in Grand Tower, Illinois, a small, southern town near the Muddy and Mississippi Rivers. His grandfather appropriately bestowed the nickname "worry wart" upon him at an early age. He was slight built as a child, but learned to stand up to the toughest boys in town.

Somehow, the worry part got dropped from his name and he was left with "Wart." He would come into the store to talk to Ollie about where they planned to go fishing or hunting on the weekend. He was handsome and friendly. He always wore crisply ironed dress pants, not jeans. There was never a hair out of place and you could see the shape of his muscular arms through his tailored shirts. Sometimes, he would help behind the meat counter slicing dozens of hams for a catering company. I would wrap the orders and we would banter back and forth about silly stuff. He had a great sense of humor.

Lavern (Wart) How at Gross Market

One day, he asked me if I wanted to take a Sunday afternoon ride with him in his shiny yellow, Mustang fastback. (It was really lime green, but I didn't find out until much later.) As we drove, he told me about his date the night before. Since we were just friends, I didn't mind. The subject matter wasn't important; I was totally smitten. He continued to flirt with me now and then. We began dating, although I couldn't believe he was interested in me since he was older and much worldlier than I would ever be. He had been in the Navy for four years and traveled to many different countries. I had never left Missouri. I laid awake at night thinking about him. In my dreams, he was the knight-in-shining-armor who rescued me from an oppressive place.

I found a full-time job at Volkswagen Insurance Company on Lindell Boulevard. I was asked to sort the insurance renewal forms that the underwriters had reviewed. If they had been changed in any way, they were to go in one stack. If they had not, they would be sent to the data processing department in another stack. Speed was essential since there were hundreds of forms to check. No problem, I thought. After flipping through about fifty papers, I took the papers to the data entry clerk.

It wasn't long before my supervisor appeared at my desk with a frustrated look on her face. "I instructed you to sort these. Why didn't you follow my directions?"

I looked at her with tears welling up in my eyes "I did. There weren't any changes."

She proceeded to show me each form, pointing to the marks made by the underwriters. I had to strain to see them. For some reason, the green ink scribbled on reprocessed paper was nearly impossible for me to see. It was then that I realized I should have told her I thought I was color blind. My first day might have been my last. Instead, the underwriters were issued red pens the next day.

Wart and I continued to see each other more often. In the fall of 1971, he asked me to come to Joplin, where he had been working. Going away for the weekend was not an acceptable thing for an unmarried woman to do. My father, after giving me his finest lecture on the type of women who do such things, told me that if I left, not to come back.

I replayed his words over and over again in my head. I loved my family, but during the past few years I had decided there had to be more to life than what I had experienced. I also felt it might be less of a burden if there was one less mouth to feed. I packed a few possessions and got into my car. Michelle stood in the front yard, sobbing, as I backed onto the street and headed to the airport. I cried the entire drive to the parking garage and on the flight down to Joplin.

Wart picked me up at the airport and he surprised me by taking me to a jewelry store where I picked out my engagement and wedding rings. We became husband and wife on New Year's Eve. By then, I was pregnant with Laura. I didn't tell anyone, except Wart. I knew I had become the terrible person my father convinced me I was. I was ashamed and embarrassed; I didn't have the courage to tell my parents or grandparents of my condition.

It wasn't hard to hide my pregnancy. I was so sick during most of the early months that I gained very little weight. I seldom saw my family, except for my brother, Rob, who had moved out when he married Lana. Wart and I bowled on a league with them and one day, they noticed my swollen ankles and asked me if I was pregnant. We let them in on our secret, and asked them to keep it quiet.

We scraped together enough money to put a down payment on a new mobile home and moved to St. Charles, just over the Highway 70 Bridge. We didn't have much, but we were determined to make it on our own.

On Friday, March 11, my supervisor called me into her office and asked me if I wanted to tell her anything. I knew she had caught on to my condition. I admitted that I was pregnant. She reminded me that company policy demanded that I give notice immediately and leave by the time I was seven months along. Although I did not look like it, I was due to deliver May 5. I should have told her then, but I needed to work as long as I could.

Saturday, Wart and I went to Winfield to fish in the Sandy Slough. The weather was clear and sunny, but cold. More importantly, the fish were biting. We stayed until midday. Wart loaded our catch into the trunk and we started for home. All of a sudden, it was as if a water balloon had burst and fluid was flowing down the seat of the car. I had no idea what was happening, but I knew it wasn't good.

The only words my mother had ever said to me about female issues were, "Here, you need this," when she handed me my first sanitary napkin. She never spoke to me about having sex, much less having a baby. Something told me that I should probably go to the hospital.

Wart took me to Christian Northwest Hospital on Hanley Road. The nurse checked me over and said, "It will be a little while."

Wart said, "What will be a little while?"

"The baby." Her response came as a shock to both of us.

Wart gave me a kiss and said, "I'll be back after I take care of some business." I figured he was going to give the fish to Ollie and come right back.

Three hours later, he walked in the labor room. He didn't tell me where he had been and I didn't ask. I didn't know he had done what I hadn't had the courage to do. He went to my grandparent's house first.

Wart always speaks his mind without sugar coating anything. I love that about him. He broke the news to my grandfather with the same honesty. "What's done is done. If you don't like it, that's too bad. We're having a baby and you will have to choose whether or not you accept us for who we are."

With that, he left and went to my parents house and told them they were about to become grandparents. My father had been drinking heavily and they exchanged heated words.

Just before they took me into delivery, my dad staggered into the room. He leaned over me, mumbled something and kissed me. He reeked of stale beer. The labor pains and drugs kept me from forming any words to comfort him. I felt sorry for him. I knew I had disappointed him greatly.

Laura was born just before midnight on March 12. Although premature, she had all the necessary working parts and weighed in at a mere four pounds, eight ounces. Since we had no insurance, they released me after two days, but kept Laura. Wart took me to the mobile home and had to return to his job site in Hannibal. He felt terrible about leaving me, but we had no choice. He was the only source of income now and we would need every bit we could scrape together to pay the bills.

I couldn't drive so I couldn't get to the hospital to see Laura. I didn't even have a phone to call and check on her. I spent the next five days feeling like the worst mother in the world. When Wart came home on the weekend, we drove to the hospital to bring our baby home. They brought out a little bundle and placed it in my arms. Wart looked at the tiny face and exclaimed: "This isn't our baby. It's a boy." Sure enough, they had brought us the wrong baby. The nurse quickly took the baby back and returned with our tiny little girl. She was beautiful and I couldn't wait to get to know her.

I didn't see my parents again for a few months. They didn't try to contact me or check to see how their new grandchild was doing. I was hurt, but I felt it was my fault. When I did get up the nerve to stop by for a visit, my father got in the car and left. Conversations with Mom were strained. She was quiet and reserved. I felt there was nothing I could say that would bridge the crater that had formed between us. It wasn't long before they moved to Pinebluff, Arkansas for a year as the result of job relocation.

My grandparents completely surprised me. They welcomed us into their home and never said a word about the past. I believe my grandfather truly appreciated the frankness and determination of my husband's words the day Laura was born. For the next few years, we visited them three or four nights a week to play Pinochle and Canasta. They delighted in seeing Laura sit in her pumpkin seat and sleep while we laughed late into the night. The minute we returned home and opened the door, she'd be awake and ready to play.

I wish we could have had the same closeness with my parents that we did with my grandparents. Things don't always work out the way you want them to, but. I am grateful for the love and friendship we shared with Non and Gramps.

Chapter Seven

A New Experience

I was a stay-at-home mom and loved it. Wart worked out of town a lot, but was at home on weekends. When we could afford it, and sometimes even when we couldn't, Laura and I would travel with him. Laura was just about a year old when Wart had an extended job in Overton, Nevada, a desert town about seventy miles from Las Vegas. Since he expected to be gone for a long time, we packed our bags and joined him.

For someone who had traveled very little, the journey was fascinating to me. I marveled as we passed prairies filled with tumbleweeds, mountains that made the hill at the club look small and pristine waters that seemed to capture the blue from the sky. Being so close to places I always wanted to visit, like Pikes Peak, was enticing and I hoped we'd have the chance to take them in on the way, but time did not allow for it. We did get to see Hoover Dam and it was magnificent.

When we traveled through the Valley of Fire, I started to become concerned about how prepared I was to live in a desert area. Armadillos and lizards roamed freely under the scorching sun. Huge red boulders were all you could see for miles. The lack of trees unsettled me and you could travel for an hour without ever seeing another car. We finally reached Overton and I felt a little more at ease. There was a post office, laundromat, and swimming pool. I even noticed a movie theatre that was open on weekends. Two small motels were located on the main street through town as was a small grocery store that had basic items like canned goods, milk and prepackaged meat, such as bacon and hot dogs.

Our rented kitchenette became home for the next five months. It was exciting and frightening at the same time. Wart and the crew worked nights because of the 115 degree temperatures during the day. When he would get off work, about six a.m., we would drive to Lake Meade and swim until the sun took over about nine a.m. Then we'd go back to the motel and sleep.

One morning as I started to open the door upon his return home from work, Wart shouted: "Don't open the door just yet." A King snake had taken up residency in front of our door.

It must have been the year of the locust. Any light left on at night was an invitation for an invasion. One night I had forgotten to turn off the bulb outside and close the windows on the car. Every locust within a hundred miles heard about it and arrived within an hour after sundown. They beat steadily on the windows of our room. It was just like a horror movie except you couldn't turn the sound off. Even though I finally turned out the light, it was too late. By morning, thousands of them had invaded the inside of the car. Wart was not a happy camper as he shoveled out mounds of leftover visitors the next morning.

Any serious grocery shopping was done in Las Vegas. About once a week, we would make the drive into town for items they didn't carry in the local store. I never made it to the Las Vegas strip, but we came close one time. Rob and Lana drove out to visit us on their vacation. Their son, Robby, was about six months old. We kept him one night so Rob and Lana could go to the casinos. While they were there, they found out that there were professional babysitting services available. The next day, we all loaded up in Rob's car and drove to Las Vegas with the intent of leaving the kids with a sitter and enjoying a few hours on the strip.

We laughed and joked all the way to town. When we pulled into a gas station to ask directions, Rob noticed something dripping under the car. The water pump was busted and so we spent the rest of the day sitting at the station getting a new pump installed. That was as close as I got to visiting the Las Vegas strip. I do remember they had slot machines in the grocery stores. I might have played a nickel a few times.

Sometime in August, Wart hurt his ankle and we ended up at the emergency room in Las Vegas. It turned out he had a fracture. He also had a staph infection so the doctor was not able to put a cast on his foot. On crutches and unable to work, we made the long drive back to St. Charles. We stopped in Glenwood Springs, Colorado and spent the night. The next day, we drove and drove, and drove. Eighteen hours later, we arrived at our mobile home in the middle of the night.

In our long absence, family members kept tabs on our mobile home. My brother-in-law, John, had turned off the electric in order to save us money while we were gone. Little did he know that we had left a can of orange juice in the freezer. It exploded from the heat. Lana, my sister-in-law, had stopped by to check on the place and was greeted with the stench. She cleaned up the mess and opened the windows to air the house out before we arrived home. What a trooper!

The screen door was locked and the only key we had to get into the house fit the front door. My resourceful husband removed one of the screens from a window and pushed me through to the other side. I would not make a good cat burglar. I landed with a loud thump and fortunately, did not break anything. The bruises on my legs remained there for about two weeks, but I was able to unlock the front door so Wart could hobble through it on his crutches. Traveling is great, but there is no place like home.

Chapter Eight

Lessons Learned

Many of the lessons learned from my parents and grandparents are the basis for the values I hold dear. Respect, honesty and a strong sense of responsibility are some of those traits that Wart and I tried to instill in Laura as she grew up. While we appreciated many of the things we were taught when we were young, the methods for delivering the lessons often differed greatly from that of my parents. We buried rules like no talking or getting out of bed at night. It wasn't always easy to break other family traditions. Some things were a struggle.

In 1977, I decided it was time to return to the working world. My mother and grandmother were not happy with my decision and reminded me of all the reasons I should change my mind. I missed being in the workforce and needed to feel useful. Laura soon would be in school full time. Against their wishes, I applied and was hired through Civil Service, at a government agency on Page Avenue in St. Louis.

The week before I was to report, we were driving west on the service road of Highway 70 heading to a department store to buy some clothes for my new job. Wart and I saw it at the same time. A cement truck, eastbound on the highway, blew out a front tire. The impact was so forceful that it lifted the truck in the air about a foot. It crashed down on the pavement with a bounce. The look of terror in the driver's eyes confirmed that he no longer had control of the monster vehicle. The multi-ton truck was headed directly toward us.

The saying "my life flashed before my eyes" had new meaning. Would we survive? If Laura survived and we didn't, who would care for her? Was I wrong to accept the job? If I live through this, but I'm injured, will they hold the job for me? I thought about all the words to loved ones that would be left unsaid.

Wart slammed the gas pedal to the floor and sped into the oncoming traffic lane of the service road, which fortunately, was empty at the time. The heavy truck left the highway and with a thunderous impact, tipped over just in front of where our car had been moments before. The force of the impact caused the chute that delivers the concrete to break free. It was coming straight toward our windshield. Laura was in the back seat and I pushed her to the floor, sure we all would be decapitated. I squeezed my eyes shut. I waited for the sound of glass breaking or metal crunching. Instead, it was suddenly quiet.

My eyes opened to see Laura climbing up onto the seat and I released the breath I had been holding. Gray dust, rocks and dirt covered the car, but we were untouched. Even the car was not permanently damaged. I looked behind us where the cement truck laid on its side. Dust was still settling when Wart got out of the car and went to see about the driver of the truck. I watched as the door of the cab was pushed open and the man climbed out. Other than being frazzled, he appeared to have no serious injuries. Wart, concerned about gas leaking on the motor, asked him if he was going to shut off the engine.

"F… that engine," was his reply.

I silently thanked God for sparing us and for giving Wart the quick reflexes to get us safely out of the way. I knew how close we had come to death or serious injury. It took a few minutes for my nerves to settle down, but soon we went on our way to finish our shopping. It took a little longer to dispel the doubts about going to work.

The next week, I reported to work and assumed my position as a file clerk. After the first two days, I decided I would have no trouble being a mother, wife and employee. By the third day on the job, Laura no longer found the new routine to her satisfaction. She threw a tantrum when I dropped her off. I put on a tough act and reassured her that she would have fun with her new playmates. In reality, the guilt threatened to consume me. I began to question my decision to put my needs before my daughter's desires.

On the fourth day, I received an emergency call from the day care. I was told to come pick her up, immediately. The nurse on duty noticed a swollen gland and thought she had the mumps. The school couldn't risk having the other children exposed. I went to my supervisor and explained the situation. She was understanding and said I could leave; however, I needed to return as quickly as possible.

I contacted the doctor and he advised me to give Laura a sour pickle test. I had never heard of it, but it was worth a try. If she had the mumps, and took a bite of the pickle, I would know it. If she ate one without complaint, she most likely did not have the mumps. She had no problem with the pickle, in fact, she ate two. I scheduled an appointment for the weekend just to be sure there wasn't anything else going on.

I called a neighbor, Mrs. Kramer, and pleaded with her to care for Laura since the daycare would not allow her to come back until she had been seen by the doctor. She obliged and we walked to her trailer. Laura burst into tears when she realized I was leaving her to go back to work. Between heart-breaking sobs, she cried, "Do you mean you can't even stay with me when I'm sick?"

I was in tears. I seriously questioned my decision to return to the workforce, but I had just started the new job and needed to fulfill the commitment I had made. I recognized that Laura was trying to use guilt to get her way.

My grandmother taught my mother guilt. I think Mom passed it onto me with a basket of clothes that needed to be folded. I decided it was time to break the cycle. With all the inner strength I could muster, I gave Laura a hug, said I was sorry, and returned to work.

All afternoon, I struggled with my decision. When I picked her up later that day, she was all giggles and smiles. She survived and so did I. It was another lesson learned.

Wart and I wanted Laura's life to be easier and more fun than what we had known. We made up many of the rules as we went along. A stern look was enough to take the place of a whipping. Talking was encouraged and so was laughing, lots of it. Most importantly, she learned to respect others, not through fear, but through our actions and words that told her we respected her, too.

Chapter Nine

The Black Cloud Theory

I have a theory that there are celestial forces that cause a black cloud to align over my head like a hovering spacecraft on a regular basis. I have no concrete proof of this theory, but it repeats itself frequently enough that I am pretty sure I am right.

I encountered this unfortunate occurrence the first time my husband had to travel without us to Louisiana for a few weeks for his job. Suddenly, I was like a single parent of our four-year-old daughter and sole caretaker of our mobile home. Always the optimist, I believed this would be a great opportunity to show I could manage both tasks successfully. The first few days weren't bad. I dropped Laura off at daycare, went to work, came home and fixed dinner. Laura whimpered at bedtime when her daddy was not there to tuck in his baby girl. The weekend came and I was oblivious to the unexplainable nebula of darkness that formed in the skies above.

Laura's blue eyes widened with excitement as she watched me push the nearly immovable coffee table across the room. An innocent look of wonder crossed Laura's face as I unfolded the full size sofa-sleeper. I had planned our little living room camp-out the night before as I tried comforting Laura to sleep. I hoped she would someday cherish the memory as much as I cherished having a sleep over at my grandparent's home when I was small. Her long blond braids bounced as she grabbed her tattered flannel blanket and her hand-me-down stuffed dog, Henry, and jumped onto the newly made bed.

I read her a story and soon she was fast asleep. Despite the metal frame from the stow-away bed poking my back and hips, I too drifted off to sleep about midnight.

Peaks and Valleys

"BAM! BAM! BAM!" I was jolted awake by what sounded like shotgun blasts which vibrated the wall near my head. It was pitch black when I jumped out of bed and slammed both shins into the anvil of a table. I probably would have paused to tend to my injuries, but my heart was pounding out of my chest with anticipation of the next round of ammo coming through the wall. I stumbled across the room and worked my trembling fingers between the slats on the tightly closed blinds, trying hopelessly to see from where the ghastly noise had come.

Silence filled the room. All I could see was the familiar trailer next door and a starlit sky above it. Anxiously, I moved from room to room checking every window in great expectation of some horrific monster with a gun. At each window I saw nothing, but peaceful moonlit yards. My breathing began to slow and my heart no longer pounded louder than the clock on the wall.

I did not imagine that noise, I told myself. I glanced at my daughter sleeping soundly and began to question my sanity even more. If the noise had been as loud as I remember, how could she still be asleep?

A few minutes passed when I heard a light rap on a distant door and a voice say, "Hey Mike, get up. The police are on the way." It was Jerry, the neighbor, from two trailers up the road trying to stir my next door neighbor. He seemed relatively calm as he walked back and forth waiting for Mike to come out.

I could not go back to bed until I knew what had happened. I quickly got dressed and decided to go outside to get an explanation. I listened as Jerry explained to Mike that he had been home from work for just a short while when he heard the engine of his new car start up. He grabbed his loaded 20-gauge shotgun and chased the would-be thieves down to my trailer where he pulled the trigger and let off a few rounds. Now I understood why the shots I heard were so close to my house. The boys had jumped out of his car and it rolled until it was stopped by Mike's car.

The only casualties from the shotgun blast were a few cars across the street which looked like they had been sandblasted. Within a few minutes, the police arrived with a canine unit and having a great fear of dogs, I excused myself to check on Laura. She was still sleeping soundly and oblivious to the excitement of the night. I put on a pot of coffee and settled down with a paperback until dawn.

By my third cup of java, the August sun began to peek through the blinds. The plan for the morning was outlined in my mind. I would surprise my husband by mowing the lawn, then take Laura to her swim lessons at the Boys and Girls Club. I waited until eight-thirty a.m. to drag the mower out from the shed. It took a few attempts of priming the bulb and pulling the cord, but I was finally able to start the push mower. I was quite proud of myself.

I had trimmed a mere twenty feet of grass before I found the discreet copper water line that was buried below the tall blades of grass. In seconds, I thought I had been transported to Yellowstone National Park as I watched a magnificent geyser erupt in front of me. I stood dumfounded, unable to move. From shock to frantic, I tried to remember where the shutoff valve might be. My husband had shown me the one in the house, but that would not help me outside. I visualized the man poking his rod down into a hole each month as he read the meter and it dawned on me that it was below ground. I looked around and spotted the deep, spider-filled opening which was barely visible through the overgrown weeds.

I dropped down to my knees, reached in and tried to find the handle. There was nothing but webs. The only way to reach the meter was to lay flat on the ground. I sprawled out, face first, and reached my arm into the hole as far as I could, trying not to think about the crawling creatures that would soon attach themselves to my skin. There was no handle. I jumped to my feet and dashed inside to call for help.

"Bill, I need your help now!" I shouted into the phone.

"Who is this?" Bill Kramer, the trailer court manager, replied.

I could have said it was the crazy, dumb blond from down the street, but instead I identified myself and gave a brief explanation of my crisis. Bill agreed to come to my rescue. When he arrived, he took one look at me and burst into laughter. There I stood, saturated from head to toe with grass clippings clinging to most of my body. He proceeded to take his wrench and stop Old Faithful as if it was another daily routine. I thanked him, knowing I would never again be able to have a conversation with him that did not involve my humiliating call.

There was just enough time for a shower and change of clothes before taking Laura to her swim lessons. An hour of watching her thrash about in the water with her friends would help me relax, I told myself optimistically. I found a place on the stadium-type bench and tucked my daughter's shoes and towel and my purse in the space underneath.

I offered a hand to the young mother who came up behind me as she struggled to unload a large diaper bag, purse, towel and an infant in a pumpkin seat. We chatted a little about her newborn. She related that she was stressed about the weather report and thunderheads she had seen building on the horizon. I assured her we were safe inside the sturdy concrete building.

After a short while, she could no longer ignore her concerns and decided to get her daughter from the pool and leave. I kept an eye on her sleeping baby as she dried off her daughter and gathered all her bags. Once she had everything balanced over her shoulder or under an arm, she picked up the pumpkin seat and left.

About thirty minutes into the lesson, I reached down to get a piece of gum from my purse. My hand grasped anxiously from side to side, but couldn't feel anything that remotely resembled a purse. I stood up and looked underneath the bench. Laura's shoes and a towel were the only things on the floor. *My purse, oh my God! My purse is gone.*

Panic sank in as I remembered my husband was out of town and no one else had keys to my car or house. I dashed to the check-in desk seeking help. My voice was quivering as I tried to get someone's attention, but the staff was too distracted by the impending storm that blackened the skies overhead.

Just as I thought I would burst into tears, the young woman who had sat next to me came rushing through the door with my purse in hand.

"I'm so sorry! I grabbed your purse when I left. I didn't realize until I got home that I had it. I left the kids with my husband and hurried back as fast as I could."

Overwhelmed with gratitude, I thanked her and headed back to the bench to once again get my blood pressure under control. The moment my derriere hit the bench, a large clap of thunder shook the building and all the lights went out. Fifty blood-curdling renditions of "MOM!" were shouted from the pool. A staff person tried to announce the emergency instructions, but could barely be heard above the shrill screams. The only back up lights available were BIC cigarette lighters held by a few shaking hands.

One by one, the children were removed from the water and returned to their anxious parents. With Laura by my side and my car keys securely in hand, we sat briefly waiting for the storm to pass. The thought of going to the trailer and riding out the storm was ruled out. I never felt safe there in bad weather even when my husband was there to calm my fears. Instead, I thought it would be a good time to visit Mom in Florissant.

The skies cleared as Laura and I made the drive to Mom's house. Mom put on a fresh pot of coffee while Laura and my youngest sister watched television. Mom and I retreated to the breezeway as I narrated a brief version of my nightmare weekend. It was great to finally relax in a secure environment. Of course, it was just a façade.

I took another sip of coffee and my eyes caught a glimpse of something outside. I studied the blacktop driveway. It was parallel to the side street and could hold about four cars comfortably if you pulled in close, perpendicular to the fence. Hadn't the car been almost touching the fence? An alarm was going off in my head. My white Ford Pinto was inching slowly backwards toward the street. I bolted from my chair, sending the coffee flying everywhere, and dashed down the dozen steps to the bottom landing. I flung open the screen door and headed for the car. I was berating myself all the way. How could I have forgotten to put it in park? Imagine my surprise when I whipped open the driver's door and found my little girl scrunched down on the floor board of the passenger side!

Once again my heart felt like I had been in a marathon race. Thank goodness the side street had little traffic and was relatively flat. I was able to apply the break and stop the car before it made it into the street. Laura knew she was in trouble, but I knew if I opened my mouth, she would get all the frustrations of the day. Instead, I buckled her in the car seat and pushed the car back into its spot. Mom was standing at the steps by then, so I asked her to keep an eye on Laura while I retrieved my purse and keys from upstairs. I was going home to lock myself away for the rest of the day.

The ride home was uneventful, thank goodness. As I unlocked the door to the trailer, I heard the phone ringing. "How's it going?" my husband asked on the other end.

"Just fine," I lied.

"Why don't you see if you can get a flight down here and take a few days off of work?"

It was music to my ears. I never knew you could book a flight, pack your bags and beg a ride to the airport in less than an hour, but I did it. By evening, Laura and I were in Louisiana driving across Lake Ponchartrain. I had finally escaped the big black cloud that rested over St. Charles.

Laura How

After three relaxing days at the beach, swimming and fishing, I returned to St. Charles. I had almost forgotten the craziness that preceded my trip, but was quickly brought back to reality when I returned to the mobile home and opened the door. A horrible, sickening smell permeated the entire house. I walked room to room expecting to find a dead body. I nearly gagged when I reached the kitchen.

Somehow, the circuit breaker for the upright freezer had tripped (probably during the storm) and pounds of burger and chuck roasts had been rotting since I left. It took days to get the smell out of the house and it was just one more piece of evidence to support my black cloud theory.

Chapter Ten

Talking to God

God had answered my prayer to keep death away from our family for a long time. Unfortunately, it was as if He had saved up twenty year's worth and dumped them on us all at once.

In 1984, Wart received a phone call telling him that his youngest brother, Monty, had been killed in a truck accident. He was only thirty-three. It was the first funeral for his family and mine in many years. Losing the youngest member of his family saddened everyone. His death was like a snow ball that turned into an avalanche.

My grandmother called me at work. Her voice quivered as she asked me to come to her house as quick as I could. My grandfather had fallen and was having difficulty standing and talking. The fifteen minutes it took to get to their house felt like an hour. As I walked into their house, I saw Gramps, sitting in his chair, looking bewildered. When he tried to talk, tears began to stream down his face and he was unable to form the words he desperately wanted to speak. I immediate called for an ambulance and he was rushed to Normandy Osteopathic Hospital.

At first the doctors insisted that he did not have a stroke, but they could not tell me what was happening. By the next day, it was obvious they were wrong. He was getting worse and soon slipped into a coma. The family gathered by his side, waiting for the inevitable. Everyone was there except Rob, who lived out of state. As if anticipating his return, Gramps held on until he and Lana arrived.

At the same time, Wart received a call telling him his step-father had died. The day of my father-in-law's funeral, my Grandfather passed from the stroke.

Almost every other week, we received a call informing us of another funeral. Wart's mother passed suddenly. Two of his uncles, his aunt and three of his friends with whom he hunted and fished also died, including Ollie Gross.

My side of the family was not untouched. Nearly all of my aunts who visited the club house each summer passed, as did a co-worker and a Girl Scout friend. It was a difficult time.

My grandmother began to show signs of dementia. Many of my visits were spent searching for her check book and other documents that she would lose nearly every day. Her doctor was more concerned with her low blood count than her inability to remember things. She would receive a blood transfusion and within a few weeks, her iron count would be low again.

A colonoscopy was ordered and during the procedure, her colon was ruptured. She was put on life support and died a few days later in May 1989. Mom felt a terrible sense of guilt for having authorized the test, but we knew she had no choice.

My father's health was continuing to decline, although he would not seek medical help. He refused to eat and spent most of his days in bed. He continued to drink his beer and smoke his cigarettes, but little else.

For Christmas, I decorated sweatshirts for each member of our family. I wrote a personal letter to each person sharing those things I found most endearing and special about his or herself. Perhaps all the deaths made me more aware of sharing those types of thoughts.

I placed dad's shirt in a box with the letter on top. The letter described all the things I admired about him and how many of the values and beliefs he passed on to me, I still cherished. I had hoped that he would know how much I loved him.

On December 27, 1989, my father passed away at Veterans Hospital from cirrhosis of the liver and cardiac arrest. When we were discussing the arrangements for his funeral, I mentioned that I was grateful that I had shared my inner most thoughts with him before he passed. Mom told me she never saw a letter in the box. She pulled it out from under the Christmas tree and we looked inside. The letter stuck to the top of the box and unfortunately, he never saw it.

Death had consumed eighteen family members and friends in a span of a few years. Once again, a black cloud hung overhead and suffocated any hint of joy from life. There were no words to describe the sadness and depression that threatened to consume our lives.

Wart no longer enjoyed going to the river to fish or hunt. The loss of so many family members made him sad beyond words. Being a man made it difficult to verbalize his sorrow.

My mother was overcome with grief. She had never been in a position to take control. Decision-making was something foreign to her and she had to deal with many legal matters. My grandparents' estate included three houses that need to be sold or managed. The one in which they had lived was now vacant and needed to be maintained. There was so much to do and yet, everything seemed unimportant. It was overwhelming.

Grief and stress took its toll on all of us. There were many days when my shoulders felt the burden of trying to be the strong, capable daughter. All of this responsibility was new to me, too, and I anguished over each decision I made.

At work, I tried to leave my personal life at the door of the office, so that I could function in a professional manner. I soon realized how difficult it was to avoid emotions that needed attention. I thought about how my father had to return to work immediately after Keith's death. How difficult it must have been to pretend nothing had happened and to resist the temptation to flee to some faraway place. I began to recognize his alcoholism as his escape from the pain that he could not release. I found a new understanding for his angry, destructive behavior.

Although there were co-workers who were kind enough to listen and empathize, I internalized most of my thoughts. No one really wants to hear about so many deaths and such feelings of despair. I found myself writing pages of despondent thoughts, which I destroyed in fear that someone would know how distraught I felt.

When I could no longer bear the weight by myself, I turned to my faith. I left work one day and drove to St. Paul the Apostle's Church, the same place that held the funerals of my brother, father, and both grandparents. It was the church where my parents had been married, where I had been baptized and received first communion and confirmation. The core of my spiritual being was born on the same ground where my great-grandfather helped to build the first St. Paul's church. It felt like the right place to be to talk with God.

I knelt down in the first pew and wept uncontrollably. I poured out every pain, every sorrow, every worry, every sin, in desperation of finding peace. When I had exhausted every tear, I prayed to God for his help.

Perhaps it was the release of all those tears, but a strange, beautiful sensation surrounded me. I felt some of the weight lift from my shoulders. My crying stopped and I could have sworn that someone had turned on a bright light. I felt better, physically and emotionally. Whatever happened, it was encouraging. My sense of hope returned and I felt I would be okay.

Chapter Eleven

A Brief Hiatus

The death of my father seemed to end the avalanche of funerals. I began to feel hopeful that life would bring a hint of joy back to our shattered family. My grandparent's houses were sold, the estate was finalized and like God often does, He opened a new door through which my mother would walk.

A grief counselor named Margaret, who was associated with the funeral home, called Mom a couple of months after the service.

"Ms. Hootselle, I don't know if you remember me from the funeral home, but I was thinking of you and wondered how you were doing?"

"I'm fine." Mom gave her typical response, the same as always. Of course, it wasn't true. She desperately needed to unload the sorrow she carried deep inside. Little did Mom know that Margaret would not give in so easily. She had experienced similar trauma in her life, losing a small child and later her husband.

Anticipating that my mother was trying to put up a good front, she continued,

"I'm surprised. After my husband died, I found myself walking aimlessly through stores. Have you found yourself doing that?"

The words were enough to crack the stoic armor that Mom had worn. She began to cry uncontrollably. Margaret listened to her for a while and suggested they set a date to talk some more. They began to meet weekly and Mom's face reflected the difference. An occasional smile would replace the empty look she often wore. Mom had someone who could help her bare the pain of being alone.

Attending Mass at St. Paul's became a weekly tradition for Mom and me. The drive from St. Charles to Florissant, then to Pine Lawn took longer than Mass, but it was worth it. Mom found she knew many of the parishioners who had been long time residents of the area and she felt at ease. We found a new home among the loving people who attended the church. My relationship with Mom grew immensely.

Laura was entering her senior year in college in Springfield, Missouri when I decided it was time to invest in a house. Wart was content to remain in our mobile home, but I had grown restless and wanted more space and a safer location to wait out storms.

For eight months, through many rainstorms, Linda Humes, our Realtor and friend, drove us neighborhood to neighborhood, in search of the right home. It was hard to find something within our budget and fitting the location we both desired.

We found a three bedroom, split-level home in St. Peters, made an offer and it was accepted. The house had been vacant for nearly a year and was in need of some major work. The roof needed to be replaced, as did the windows and siding, but we managed to invest the time and money to make it our home.

A month later, St. Paul's church was forced to close because of declining membership and the cost of maintaining the building. The parish was merged with Ascension Church in Normandy and became known as Ascension-St. Paul.

Mom and I were very sad to watch the church that we both had come to appreciate, be sold, but the decision to join the merger was easy to make. The members had become like family and the new location was a few miles closer.

There were challenges in merging two long-established churches. Change is always hard and the age of the members made it even more difficult because each church had traditions and committees that were forced to transform. I wanted to help in any way I could.

Joining the Liturgy Committee and becoming a lector gave me an opportunity to become more involved in the merger and to experience my religion in a new light. I grew very fond of the church staff, nuns and priests.

Mom and I found many ways to become involved. My mother frequently created floral arrangements for the altar, serviced the linens and helped in the kitchen at special events. She even volunteered for the Friday fish fry events during Lent, which was one of the few times she ventured out on her own. We both helped decorate the church for Easter and Christmas services. It wasn't long before we felt at home in the new church.

In January 1999, Pope John Paul II made a pastoral visit to St. Louis. A busload of parishioners, including myself, traveled to the Trans World Dome for a Eucharistic Celebration with His Holiness. Part of me felt the showiness of most events related to the Vatican was ostentatious, but words cannot adequately describe the experience I encountered.

More than a hundred thousand people celebrated Mass with the Pope. The procession of clergy included one thousand priests, and two hundred and fifty cardinals, archbishops and bishops, dressed in cream-colored vestments. I watched in awe as they made their way slowly into the center of the dome. When the white Popemobile entered, the applause was thunderous and it brought unexpected tears to my eyes.

From the thought-provoking homily to the uplifting music, everything was done to perfection. There was such solemnity, even during the distribution of communion. I was moved much more than I had anticipated I would be. It was difficult to explain to anyone who had not been there.

Yet, I couldn't help question the extravagant expense of the event when just a few months later, another series of church closings was announced. The cost of keeping the doors of Ascension-St. Paul open exceeded the generous donations from the small parish. Once again, the church in which Mom and I had grown so comfortable would close. This time there would be no merger. Parrish members were encouraged to join a nearby church or one in our respective community. While the staff and members of the church had a beautiful and memorable closing ceremony, it felt much like another death in many ways. Searching for a new *home* would be difficult.

Chapter Twelve

The Girl Scout Experience

Girl Scouts has been prevalent in my life since Laura joined while in first grade. By her second year in Scouting, I became a leader of a Brownie Troop. I didn't know a thing about leading a group of girls, but there were plenty of resources available that helped me learn. A whole new world opened up to both of us.

Pat Vogt, Joni Wood and the late, Mary Schumacher, encouraged and mentored me as I began to chair committees and take on new roles. They saw a leadership quality in me that I had not yet discovered. As I succeeded in each position, my confidence grew and so did my self-esteem. It wasn't long before I was the Neighborhood Chairperson.

Later, I was nominated and accepted the position of District Chairperson over Warren, Lincoln and St. Charles counties. Girl Scouts provided me with a low-risk opportunity to speak and to lead. I found I had ideas and knowledge to share with others and I learned to document those skills to advance me in the workforce. The rewards were more than I could ever pay back.

Laura blossomed as she bridged from a Brownie to a Junior Girl Scout. She learned to set goals and achieve them. Her rewards were abundant as she was selected to attend events across the country. She spent two weeks horseback riding in Wyoming, backpacked the primitive island, Isle Royale, in Minnesota, and climbed Mount St. Helen in Washington.

Laura had more self-confidence by the time she was sixteen than I did at thirty. Her father can take credit for teaching her to stand up for what she believed in and to not give into peer pressure. Our hearts were full of pride when we walked across the stage with her as she was presented with the Gold Award, the highest recognition earned by a Girl Scout.

One of the best parts of Scouting, for both of us, was meeting other Scouts who became lifelong friends. My co-leader for many years, Judy Dodson, and I often took our troop camping at Camp Tuckaho in Troy, Missouri. We watched the girls grow from timid young Junior Scouts, who were afraid of the dark, to capable young adults, who had the skills needed to primitive camp and backpack wooded trails.

Judy and I often volunteered for outdoor functions together. Once, we agreed to be Unit Leaders for a group of girls at a Jamboree held at Camp Cedarledge in Pevely, Missouri. It is a beautiful camp on 700 acres about 45 minutes from St. Louis. I had visited the campground a few times, but was not familiar with many of the units.

We arrived at the check-in station on a Friday afternoon and received our instructions. The girls would not arrive until Saturday morning, so it would give us some time to become familiar with the layout of the camp and our site.

Our unit was the Glen. It consisted of nine platform tents positioned on a rocky hillside, which was densely wooded with towering trees. Judy and I decided to occupy the tent closest to the kitchen shelter as it was nearest to the parking lot. The tents were barely visible through the massive oaks and cedars. Judy and I climbed the hillside to check out all the units before preparing our bedrolls.

It was near dusk when we started. As we hiked along the steep hillside, Judy proudly showed me a new flashlight that she had purchased for the trip. We had made it to the last tent when darkness consumed every ounce of light. You literally could not see your hand in front of your eyes. Judy turned on her flash light and we slowly started following the faint trail back to our tent. We had only gone a few feet when Judy's light flickered and went out.

There we stood, frozen in place, unable to take a step with any confidence that we would not tumble down the steep terrain. The thought of spending the night sitting in the dark did not appeal to either of us. We finally inched forward a step, held our breath, and when we were sure of our foothold, we took another step. It was at least an hour before we made our way back to the bottom of the hill. The darkness was so overwhelming I could not relax enough to sleep all night. I think Judy felt the same.

There were twenty-eight campers assigned to our unit and most of them had never camped overnight. I knew we were in for a challenging couple of days. As the girls arrived, we allowed them to decide on which tent they would occupy, noting there could be only four girls in each one. Before long, they had their gear stowed away and were off to participate in the planned activities for the day, all of which were in another location.

In the dining hall, after dinner, the girls were given the choice to return to the Glen or stay in the dining hall for a few hours to play games and visit with the other campers. A staff person would escort them back to our unit later in the evening. Eight girls decided to return to the unit with Judy and I. On the walk back to the Glen, Judy noticed the thunderheads building overhead. "God, please don't let it storm," she whispered just loud enough for me to hear.

It was still daylight so it was easy for the girls to find their tents when we returned to the Glen. The sound of laughter and giggling echoed throughout the woods. Suddenly, we heard a high pitched scream coming from one of the units. Judy and I dashed up the hillside to the source of the noise. One of girls pointed to the floor where a couple of crickets danced around merrily. We tried to calm the virgin camper, telling her that the critters were just part of nature, but she wasn't buying it.

Judy and I talked it over and decided there was one empty unit available and we would move the four girls to that unit. We loaded up all of their gear and made the move. I guess the girls had decided there was safety in numbers because they stopped at the tent where the other four girls were straddled across their cots talking. They decided to remain there until the girls came back from the dining hall. That was fine with us.

Just as we were about to leave, one of the girls handed us a rubber boot that we forgot to put by her cot. We said we would make sure it was moved to the new location for her. Judy and I worked our way across the steep terrain to deliver the wayward boot. Both of us were armed with wide beamed flashlights and extra batteries this time.

"Let's take one last look to be sure there are no crawling creatures in this one," I suggested. We shined the lights under the bed, in the corners and lastly, on the wood beam that stretched across the opening of the tent. A bug was dangling from a web on Judy's side of the tent. I passed the boot to Judy.

"See if you can reach that bug with this." Judy stretched and took a swipe at the web. A humongous, hairy arm stretched down and grabbed the critter from the web. We almost screamed! I had never seen such a huge spider. Was it a Wolf Spider or a Tarantula? We couldn't tell, regardless, it was enormous.

Unsure of what we were going to do about the situation, we hiked back down to the kitchen shelter and sat on a bench to talk it over and wait for the other girls to arrive. There were no more tents available. There were only two cots in our tent and there were four girls. There wasn't enough room in the car. The only thing we knew for sure was that if the girls returned to the tent with the extra visitor, there would be no sleeping by any of the girls or us that night.

Within a few minutes, the rest of the girls arrived and made their way back to their respective tents. We listened to them chatter quietly as we sat there watching the rain start to fall.

Judy looked up toward the sky and said half jokingly, "OK God, you can let it rain. Just get rid of the darn spider!"

With that, the skies opened up and the rain pounded on the shelter's roof.

I leaned over and looked upward. "You know, God, I don't think she meant to drown us." We laughed so hard my stomach hurt.

When the rain let up, Judy and I grabbed our trusty flashlights and hiked the path to check on each unit. When we arrived at the unit where the girls had been visiting, we found all eight of them stretched across four cots that had been pushed together. They were sound asleep. Although it was against the rules, we made the decision to leave them sleep together, in hopes that we, too, could get some shut eye.

The next morning, the girls found the humongous spider still hanging from the rafter. Maybe it was the fact that it was daylight and they had survived their first night at camp, but instead of being frightened, they were excited to see it and very interested in watching it. Breakfast was served in the dining hall and the day's activities transpired without any additional challenges.

The parents began arriving Sunday afternoon to pick up the girls and one of the dads walked over to the pathway that led up to the tents. He grinned and said, "Yep, it's still there."

I responded, "What is still there?" He pointed out a snake whose head was poking out from a rock that was just inches from the path we had traveled all weekend. I was thankful it had chosen to hide discreetly until the campers left and I was even happier to return the Glen to Mother Nature.

Judy and I did not volunteer to be unit leaders at a Jamboree again, but we had plenty of other great experiences at camp. I am a life-time member and am still trying to pay back all the blessings that I have received from Scouting. I know I'll never achieve that, but it is fun trying.

Chapter Thirteen

September 11, 2001
A Day to Remember

The music on the radio began to play at five a.m. just like any other weekday morning. As I attempted to get ready for work, a migraine headache that had started sometime during the night, caused me to rest on the edge of the bed. The pounding between my temples and the nausea churning in my stomach sent me back to the comfort of my pillow for some relief.

The phone rang and woke me from my sleep. The handset was on the nightstand next to me and I reached for it.

"Hello."

"Good! You're there. Don't go to work! Turn on the television." I recognized my husband's voice on the other end.

"What is going on?" Sitting on the end of the bed, I pushed the button on the remote.

There was no need for my husband to answer to my question. The news reporter was frantically describing how a plane had crashed into the north tower at the World Trade Center. In disbelief, I watched the scene replay, over and over.

"What a terrible accident," I said, my heart already aching for the hundreds of people who would die from the impact. Wart was watching from the television in his boss's office. As he tried to fill me in on what he knew, a second plane crashed into the south tower. We both sensed immediately that this was not a freak accident. Terrorists were attacking.

There was an urgency to hear my daughter's voice. I called her at her place of work and talked to her briefly. When she hung up, I tried to reach my mother. By then, the telephone service was swamped with other people who probably also felt the same need to contact their loved ones and be reassured that everyone was safe.

I watched as men and women covered their eyes and mouth, running from the building. Others were standing nearby watching the buildings burn. Within an hour, the south tower began to collapse, floor by floor, disintegrating in slow motion. It was horrible watching it happen and knowing it could not be stopped. Onlookers ran screaming and crying, fleeing for their lives.

Billows of smoke rose from everywhere and consumed any light from the sky. When the dust began to settle, only ashes and unrecognizable debris remained. Fire fighters and police, who had charged into the burning, crumbling buildings, disappeared. Even their fire trucks and emergency vehicles were obliterated by debris. The north tower fell shortly afterward.

Meanwhile, the fear of more planes crashing into other buildings was overwhelming. A thousand questions ran through my mind. How many other Federal buildings were targeted? How many planes were hijacked? Could terrorist strikes include my worksite in St. Louis? Would the government be able to stop the hemorrhaging before thousands more were killed? When would the destruction stop? Would it go on for days ahead? Were we at war?

It was no longer a remote tragedy on television that would move me to feel brief compassion, but cause me to change the channel to avoid the uncomfortable feelings of watching more. The Department of the Army was my employer and when they announced that a plane crashed into the Pentagon, I began to sob out loud. Over the years I had walked the halls of that building many times. Now, my comrades were under attack. Was there any place that was safe?

The unprecedented order was given that all planes were grounded until further notice. It was hoped that this action would help the controllers determine how many planes were hijacked. United Airlines Flight 93, as it was reported later, was the sole plane that did not respond to the order. The heroic efforts of passengers on that plane probably saved the lives of thousands of others on the ground. When they tried to take back control of the plane, it would cost them their lives.

Like so many others, I was consumed by the television coverage. It was difficult to focus on anything else. I didn't think of it as history in the making, at that time, but life in the United States would never be the same. The security of our country had been compromised. We had been attacked on our own land. Would we ever feel safe again?

Life changed for all Americans after 9/11, especially for Federal employees. Every day when I went to work I was reminded of the catastrophe as I had to maneuver around the newly constructed concrete barriers that led to the guarded gate. Long lines of cars formed onto Page Avenue as trunks were opened and back seats were searched in every car entering the compound.

Going through the metal detectors was no longer a routine measure either. There was a new appreciation for security training and briefings. Identification badges were prominently worn, not hidden in pockets, and any unaccompanied briefcase was cause for alarm.

The thing about tragedies in the United States is that most American people extend a hand emotionally, physically and financially. The families of the victims are embraced and encouraged by complete strangers through words of hope, faith and love. Busy people with problems of their own extend a hand knowing someone would be there for them, if the situation was reversed. Hearing all of the compassionate stories made me proud to be an American. I prayed that we would never experience another attack such as this one.

Chapter Fourteen

Aloha

Flying became an unpopular mode of transportation following September 11, 2001. For four days, no flights were authorized by the Federal Aviation Authority in hopes that the security of the airways would be returned. Laura was scheduled to fly to Hawaii on one of the first flights to go out on the fifth day.

She worked for Monsanto and had made many trips to the islands over the previous two years. The journey that took her so many miles away had always caused me a twinge of anxiety. Now it caused me great stress. Although I wished she would cancel the trip, I knew she would not allow the events of the past week to prevent her from doing her job.

The night before she left, she had a brief discussion with her Dad that left me even more apprehensive.

"If I knew my plane was being hijacked, I think I would have to do something, just like the people on Flight 93."

I didn't want to hear those words, but I knew them to be true to her character.

"Damn right," Her dad replied. Nothing more needed to be said.

The next morning, Laura called me at work from the airport. She was pleased to tell me she had been bumped up to first class because there were so few people on the flight. She would be sitting in the first row. It was not what I wanted to hear. I tried not to let my imagination take me to fearful places.

Laura asked if I would give her Wart's cell phone number. He had recently been issued the phone by his employer and I could not find the number in my purse. I told her I would try to get it and call her back. After numerous attempts to obtain it, I had to call and tell her I didn't have it. She said "Okay. Tell him I love him and I'll call when I arrive in Maui."

The guilt of not being able to give her the phone number for her dad wore on me as the day went on. What if something happened and she never got to say her last goodbye?

By evening, I was a nervous wreck. Her arrival time came and went with no phone call. I was near tears and imagined the worse. Shortly after we retired to the bedroom, the phone rang. It was Laura's voice on the other end and I was relieved. Her flight had been delayed because of the newly implemented security measures that had been put in place. She was safely on the ground and all had gone well.

Not long after that trip, Monsanto offered Laura a permanent position in Maui and she accepted it. She sold the house she owned in O'Fallon, Missouri and purchased a condo just two blocks from the ocean in Kihei on the island of Maui.

It was difficult to have my only child, my best friend, so far away. On the other hand, her relocation provided me with a new escape. Every winter, when icicles hung from the gutters of our split level home and cold winds blew though the warmest of mackinaws, I would pack my bags and spend a couple of weeks basking in a tropical paradise with my daughter.

Laura often had to work so I used the time sit on the beach and write. Kama'ole Beach became my favorite spot. It was within walking distance of Laura's condominium and provided the inspirational surrounding I needed to let the words spill freely from my pen. This is one of the many entries from my journal that I scripted during a delightful stay.

The ocean has a way of dictating who is in command. Its overwhelming, seductive strength is disguised under majestic white foam that quietly swirls about on the smooth, sandy beach. When I step into its grasp, I feel its forces as it pushes me away, and then grabs hold of my legs to draw me near again.

I foolishly plant my feet firmly in the sand believing I am in control. It eliminates my stronghold without as much as a whisper. I am left floundering in a bottomless sea until it gently sets the sand back down and begins the dance again. Just when I think I have memorized its rhythm, it changes course and engulfs another foot of the beach.

I learn quickly not to turn my back to it, lest it catch me by surprise. Its undercurrent beckons deep respect. Even bold footprints along the shore are unable to resist its mighty force, for soon they will vanish even quicker than they were made, leaving every grain of sand as the ocean commands. Only fools are unimpressed by the greatness of the sea.

Wart, whose tolerance of airplanes disappeared long before 9/11, as the result of too many business flights to Alaska, joined me on one of the trips. To say he hated to fly is an understatement. Being the optimist that I am, I ordered the plane tickets hoping that he would muster the courage to fly to Hawaii with me. He refused to commit in advance, so the morning of our departure, I still wasn't sure he would join me. I had packed his bags for him and put them in the car. I feared he would back out when we arrived at the airport, but he relented begrudgingly.

A couple drinks at the bar before we boarded helped him settle down for the long journey. He survived the flight and by the third day on the island, he began to relax and enjoy himself. That is when he asked me why we had not scheduled a longer stay.

One of the most exciting things we did during our visit was to take a ride on a submarine to the ocean's floor. Not only did Wart surprise his daughter by making the journey, he fulfilled my dream of walking hand-in-hand with him on the beach under starry skies. I dream of returning there someday.

Chapter Fifteen

Tested Again

I was thrown into supervision about eight years into my career. I say thrown because I equate it to being thrown to the wolves. Well, maybe not completely, but there are enough challenges that come along with the position that left me drained when the day was done. As the result of a reduction in force, I was offered a position as a Branch Chief with the Army Discharge Review Board in St. Louis. It was take it or leave. I needed a job, so the rest is history.

It was a rough transition, but I found my leadership and organizational skills afforded me an opportunity to influence my work environment in a positive way. Within a year, our office was recognized by the Total Quality Management (TQM) Program for successfully reducing a process that often took three years to accomplish to one that was completed in thirty days. It opened new doors for me. I became a facilitator for TQM and was selected to be a trainer of a program for first line supervisors.

The stressful pace of managing a high volume office often left me looking for brief diversions. Kathy Passanise, a former co-worker who also was displaced during the reduction in force and was hired by another agency in the same building, providing my most enjoyable diversions. Over the years, we had become the best of friends.

Kathy was a few years older than me, although her playful personality made her appear much younger. She was a smart and dedicated employee who could complete work in half the time it took her peers. Her sometimes questionable sense of humor kept her office in stitches and she was loved by most who worked with her.

Kathy was passionate about dogs and volunteered at the Animal Protection Association where she was once named Volunteer of the Year. Somehow, she managed to convince me to help at the yearly dog walk in Forest Park even though I had a strong fear of dogs.

Kathy had many health issues that caused her to be in excruciating pain most of the day, but few knew it. She also was hearing impaired. She read lips very well, but using a phone created many frustrating moments for her.

The problem wasn't with Kathy. Rather, the problem was with anyone who was unfamiliar with receiving calls through services such as Relay Missouri. Many times when she was trying to make a medical appointment or speak to a doctor, the person on the other end would hang up or refuse to talk to the operator. I became her voice and a confidant.

She visited my home often and became part of my family. She got my jokes, which was my first clue that we were meant to be friends. Her quick wit was endearing and warmly accepted by my husband and daughter. She had a child-like attitude toward life and together we experienced many laughs and good times.

Kathy had a way of cheering the blues out of a bad mood. We met in the cafeteria every day for lunch with two other friends, Mary Slimer and Stella Czerniewski. Mary was a quiet, unassuming woman who listened more than talked. She had a great sense of humor, a giving heart and often took on the role of receptionist for Kathy, whenever I was not available to make phone calls. I loved to hear her honest, hearty laugh whenever Kathy chose to entertain us with one of her many stories.

Stella was joyous and warm hearted too, perhaps the reason we all became friends. She was the one who would step up and take charge whenever an unfamiliar face was seen in the cafeteria. She was the hostess that explained all the options available, pure of heart and spiritual to the core. That was Stella, ready and willing to help anyone at anytime.

In late November, 2003, Mary did not show up for work, which was very unusual for her. Kathy worked in the same office as Mary and had not heard anything about her absence. At lunch, Stella told us she had spoken with Mary over the weekend and found out she was in the hospital. She had been diagnosed with endometrial cancer and it was terminal. Mary was only forty-six years old. The news saddened us beyond words.

Mary never left the hospital and within a month, she passed. Her death came as a shock to all of us. We had all become very close friends.

Stella was diagnosed with stage four colon cancer shortly afterward, although she did not tell Kathy and I until we questioned her severe weight loss some months later. Every day she came to work, put on her best face, laughed with us at lunch and never showed the slightest hint that anything was wrong. She was firm in her determination to beat the cancer. She went through every treatment offered and held onto each small improvement, praying that one day she would be able to tell us she was cancer free. She fought hard for two years, but it was evident the horrible disease was going to win the battle.

Meanwhile, things weren't any better at home. My Mom had moved in with my husband and me because she had progressed into the late stages of Alzheimer's disease. She could no longer care for herself. The decision proved to be a great relief for me since I was trying to maintain two households, in addition to working and laying awake most nights worrying about her safety.

Having Mom nearby meant we could enjoy more time together. Wart was very supportive and did whatever he could to make it easier. I had no choice except to take Mom to an adult daycare center during the day while I worked. Wart would bring her home.

Mom was very fond of Wart and somehow she adjusted to the daily routine. She would sit patiently watching for his car and the minute he walked into the center, she would jump up from her chair and practically run to his side. When they arrived home, Wart would put on a pot of coffee and find a sweet snack for Mom. When the pot finished brewing, she'd pour him a cup of coffee to show her gratitude. It might end up in the sugar bowl or the creamer, but sometimes, she'd get it right and she was so pleased with herself.

Dropping Mom off in the morning was a different story. She was unhappy about not being able to stay at our house by herself and she didn't hide her disappointment from me. By the time I would get her inside the building, I felt overwhelmed with guilt for forcing her to spend the day where she did not want to be. It reminded me that she never wanted me to have a career or work outside the home. If I didn't have a job, I could stay home and allow her to be happier in a familiar environment.

Larry and Michelle set up a schedule where they took turns coming to the house one night a week so Wart and I could have some time to ourselves. It helped to have a little down time from the responsibility of caring for Mom.

Rob and Larry, and their wives, helped to empty Mom's home and prepare it for sale so that the money would be available for her care when needed. Their efforts were truly a labor of love as the house was in serious need of repair and had thirty years of clutter filling the rooms.

One morning in late January, she went into the bathroom and I heard a loud thump. I rushed to check on her. When I pushed open the bathroom door, she was crumpled up in a small pile near the tub. There was blood gushing from a wound on her forehead and she was unconscious. I called 911 and applied pressure to the area while waiting anxiously for the paramedics. She was taken to the hospital, treated and released a few days later. Within a week, she had another fainting spell and was back in the hospital again. Her doctor told us it was time for her to be under twenty-four hour care.

We were blessed that the house sold quickly. Rob, and his wife Lana, who had been in town nearly a month, visited nursing homes and narrowed the search to two. They allowed me to make the final decision and I picked the one closest to my house as I expected I would be the one visiting her the most.

Craig, Larry, Rob, Michelle, Mom, Diane, Carol in the courtyard at the NHC Nursing Home

I think it took me longer to adjust to Mom moving into a nursing home than it did for her. While she was not happy with her new environment, I knew she was safer. It broke my heart to watch her slip further and further into the dark world of dementia. I prayed that she was not in pain and that she knew how much her children loved her.

Amid all the chaos, there was a bright note. My daughter was preparing to move back from Hawaii, where she had lived for four years, and she purchased a home in Wentzville, just twenty minutes from our house. I was grateful she would be back in the continental U.S. and so close to us once again.

Stella lost her battle with cancer and was buried on January 28, 2007. I remember the date very well. Immediately following the funeral, I drove Kathy to an oncologist where she received the prognosis of terminal endometrial cancer. It was like a nightmare from which I couldn't wake up.

Kathy struggled emotionally and physically for the next two months. Many friends stepped forward and helped with her care. Kathy assigned another dear friend, Nancy Grove, and me co- Power of Attorney for her health care and financial decisions. She also appointed us as co-executives for her estate upon her death. I had the same responsibility for my mother and it came with a heavy heart and strong sense of responsibility.

Our goal was to keep Kathy in as little pain as possible and reassured that we would do everything we could to make her final days as comfortable as possible. She feared being alone when she died, so we also wanted to be sure someone she knew was with her all day and night. It was not possible for either of us to accomplish that without a great deal of help.

When the request went out to friends to help, it was like watching an army of angels appear at Kathy's bedside. All the years of caring for others was returned to Kathy in her final days. Nancy practically lived at the hospital and hired an extra nurse to be at her side. I could not begin to name all the people who gave freely of their time, but it was a true testament to the love that Kathy had given others. Kathy passed on March 28, 2007.

Kathy's ailing father also died within the month, as did three other friends of my family. As if that wasn't enough, my youngest sister's husband took his life a few months later that same year. The loss of so many people, who were a significant part of my life, left me feeling sad and empty.

Although it was a difficult time, my faith had already been tested some years before and a part of me knew that I was strong enough to get through another painful period of my life.

Chapter Sixteen

Who Accelerated the Treadmill?

Like many people, I often feel like I am on an endless treadmill that never slows down. Part of me thrives on the fast pace of life, but sometimes, I suspect someone tampered with the speed control, especially from Thanksgiving until Christmas, and it gets stuck in overdrive. There is never enough time to get everything done and before you know it, the season has passed like a fast moving train. The year 2009 broke the record.

I began to notice the increased speed the week of Thanksgiving. I just settled into bed when the phone rang. The nightshift nurse at the National Health Care (NHC) nursing home advised me that my Mom was found on the floor in someone else's room. It was normal for Mom to wander in and out of rooms and to be found sitting on the floor where she seemed to be planting flowers. This time, when the nurse tried to get her to stand up, she was not able to do so on her own.

I had just come from seeing Mom a few hours before and she was fine. She was as fine as a person who is in the final stages of Alzheimer's could be. I threw on some jeans and a sweatshirt, kissed my husband goodbye and made the twenty minute drive to the nursing home in less than 10 minutes.

Mom was sleeping on her bed when I arrived. Her doctor had been called by the staff. His recommendation was that she be taken to the hospital for x-rays to be sure nothing was broken. Mom had broken a hip some years ago. Ever since that surgery, she showed signs of dementia, although the doctors insisted the two were not related.

The paramedics arrived within the hour and transported per to the hospital. I followed closely behind hoping that nothing was seriously wrong.

The results from the x-rays showed a hairline fracture of her hip. The Emergency Room doctor indicated that the fracture would not require surgery. Mom would be kept overnight for observation to be sure she did not also injure her head when she fell. Since Mom was resting comfortably, I returned home about seven a.m., took a shower and crashed onto the bed hoping to get a few hours of sleep before returning to the hospital.

I no more than dozed off when the ringing of the phone woke me. I looked at the clock on the bedside table. It was seven-forty-five a.m. Another doctor, the orthopedic surgeon, was calling to discuss Mom's surgery, which he was scheduling for the following day. Confused and groggy, I questioned what I had just heard.

"I don't understand. The ER doctor said no surgery would be required. "

The voice on the other end of the phone drew a breath and proceeded, "Without surgery, she will have to remain in bed for at least two months in order for the break to heal. During that time, she will be in terrible pain and the chance of infection is very high."

Mom had a strong desire to roam and there was no conceivable way to keep her immobile for two months. The nursing home policy would not allow restraints. I had no choice. Reluctantly, I agreed to the surgery notwithstanding my fears that the effects of anesthesia would send her further into the darkness of her dementia.

It didn't take much more than a few hours after surgery for my fears to be validated. Mom was more confused than ever. She could no longer feed herself and didn't seem to understand anything that was said.

She remained in the hospital a few days before returning to the nursing home to heal. Physical therapy was scheduled for three days a week. My new daily routine included working forty hours, being available for as many meals and therapy sessions as possible, and anything else I could squeeze into twenty-four hours. The treadmill was in overdrive.

Thank goodness for Wart. I don't think we would have had a warm meal if it hadn't been for him. He had been forced into retirement earlier in the year so he pitched in and kept up with the laundry, shopping and house cleaning while I tried to be Florence Nightingale.

My brother, Larry, and sister, Michelle, helped with the daily feedings and visits with Mom, too. It was a challenge for all of us to keep up with the schedule, but we knew the staff at the nursing home was limited and they could not provide her with the extra attention we felt she needed.

Mom could not comprehend the changes that had transpired since the surgery. She did not like being fed by anyone and had no intention of being confined to a wheelchair. Her persistence in trying to walk on her own resulted in three falls over the next two weeks. The last one injured her hand although she continued to move it as if she was not in much pain. She used it often to shoo me away from trying to feed her.

Thank goodness I had scheduled vacation for the week of Christmas. I can remember when I gave notice to my boss; I thought (smugly) that this was one year where I would be so organized that Martha Stewart would be envious. Many of my thoughts like that are flawed, but I convinced myself that things would slow down to a more manageable pace with all that free time. There would be no reason I could not host a family dinner for twenty-five people and be an attentive daughter too. Perhaps a normal person would have reconsidered, but not this eternal optimistic. I was determined to follow through on my commitment. *I'll just kick the speed up on the treadmill*, I thought.

When we got the phone call on Saturday morning telling us my brother-in-law, John, had passed away, I faltered slightly. Although John had been ill for some time, it was unexpected and a very difficult loss. My husband was especially close to him and was his fondest fishing and hunting partner. The funeral took place on Monday. The cold rain during the service at the National Cemetery was appropriate for the somber occasion. Family gathered afterward at Wart's sister's home. Dark clouds lingered overhead and within our hearts.

Laura and her boyfriend, Daniel, were leaving for South Carolina later in the week to visit his parents for Christmas. We had decided some weeks prior that we would celebrate Christmas early with them about five p.m. on Tuesday evening. Laura called to remind me that we also had agreed to keep their sixty pound Labrador while they were gone. She asked if it would be okay to drop him off on Wednesday evening about six p.m. A saner person would have backed out right then, but he is our grand-dog and some part of me just can't say no once I have said yes. Besides, I thought, how much trouble could a young pup be?

Laura and Hammie

Tuesday morning Wart and I were loading the groceries into the car, amidst the persistent rain, when my cell phone rang. The nurse from NHC was calling to ask if anyone had told me that Mom had an appointment at two p.m. to see the orthopedic surgeon for her wrist. Of course, no one had told me. It was now twelve p.m. The shuttle would arrive at the home at 1:00 p.m. to pick her up. I needed a miracle to be able to accompany her, but I told the nurse I could be there, no problem.

We dashed home and dropped off my husband and the carload of groceries. I decided the fastest route would be to take the highway. Wrong. Two lanes were shut down for construction. I wanted to cry although I knew that wouldn't help. I turned the radio up and listened to the announcer remind me that Christmas was just three days away. It was just what I needed to send my stress level into the red zone.

I managed to arrive at the nursing home at the same time as the shuttle. I rushed in to find Mom lying on her bed half naked. No one had gotten her dressed and the home's policy dictated that whenever residents were in bed, they are stripped from the waist down. I was fit to be tied, but didn't want to upset Mom so I put on my best smile, grabbed some clothes from the closet and struggled to pull the stretch pants over her bare legs. It was difficult because her leg was still sore from the hip surgery. Thankfully the transporter was patient enough to wait for us.

Mom fussed all the way to the appointment because she hated being shuttled around like an invalid. She tolerated the x-rays which revealed a hairline break in her hand. The doctor and I discussed the possibility of surgery, but we agreed that it was not in her best interest since the pain did not appear to be severe and she was still using her hand. He didn't bother to wrap it since he suspected she would pull the bandage off quicker than it was applied.

Since Mom was already in the doctor's office, the surgeon decided it was time to remove the staples from the hip surgery. She was irritated and fuming by the time he finished and the shuttle arrived to take us back. It was about five p.m. when we arrived at NHC. Mom was exhausted. No sooner did she get settled in bed, she was asleep. I headed home just in time to sit in the rush hour traffic.

Wart had taken care of most everything. He baked the lasagna, tossed the salad and had the breadsticks warming in the oven. Laura and Daniel had already arrived and I walked in just in time to enjoy a relaxing dinner. We exchanged gifts and caught up on the day's events before they headed back to their house.

Wednesday was dog proofing day. Now, it is one thing to child proof a house, but when you have an ambitious, inquisitive, long legged, trouble-seeking furry friend, you leave no counter or table top to chance. There is no corner of the kitchen floor that has not been taste-tested by this dog. Our house does not have a room where you can easily contain a pup that has not learned to "leave it." In the back of my mind, I wondered if they make big doggie playpens. Something told me I was going to need one.

I left the house at least three times during the day, Wednesday, to help Mom with her meals, attend a care plan meeting, and to complete last minute Christmas shopping. Each time I came back with wet hair and shoes. It seemed the rain would never stop.

Hammie arrived as planned. Normally, the dog is glued to Wart's side. Unfortunately, as soon as Laura and Daniel left, my husband retired to the bedroom and closed the door. He had been feeling poorly and was not in the mood to handle the playful behavior of our guest. It wasn't long before Hammie had to make his first trip out to the yard to do his duty. I dreaded this because I knew he would return ankle deep in mud.

I had towels and a rug lying on the floor, prepared to catch him when he came through the door. Hammie had other ideas. He dashed past me and began racing around the dining room table as if he were a greyhound instead of a lab. He made about ten laps before I could catch him. The floor looked like Churchill Downs after the Kentucky Derby. Armed with towels and carpet cleaner, I got down on my hands and knees to scrub up the messy sludge before my husband saw it and went into spasms. Hammie took my position as an invitation to play and all sixty pounds of him pounced on my head. It was going to be a long week.

Thursday, Christmas Eve, was dedicated to getting the roasts cooked, brownies baked and anything else I could do ahead of time to get things in order for Christmas dinner. In between baking and roasting, I visited Mom twice. She seemed agitated with the extra attention at meal time. One of the staff offered to help her so I accepted and cut the visit short.

Wart was tired from Hammie's many trips in and out to the yard in my absence. The rain had not stopped so the routine still required the physical tackling to wipe his paws. When I got home, it wasn't long before Wart returned to the bedroom. Unknowingly, he left the bedroom door ajar. Hammie wandered down the hall and noticed the opportunity at hand (or snout, in his case). He pushed his long black nose hard enough through the crack to open the door. With one quick leap, he jumped up on the bed and joined his buddy.

I decided to take advantage of the opportunity to run downstairs and put in a load of laundry. I moved the plastic gate that kept Hammie from exploring the lower level of our home, took one step, turned around to put the gate back in its place and the next thing I knew, I was tumbling headfirst down the rest of the stairs to the landing. The railing tore the skin on my right hand as I tried to control the fall. I landed with a crash on my left wrist and tail bone. The noise was enough to bring Hammie and my husband racing into the room.

They both stood at the top of the stairs looking at me in disbelief. There I sat on the landing with one hand bleeding and the other bent in an unusual angle. Hammie was too frightened to cross the gate that had fallen. He just sat there with his sad eyes, whimpering pathetically. Wart offered to get me to my feet, but I chose to remain sitting as I was in too much pain to move. Eventually, I got up and hobbled up the stairs.

My wrist was already swelling like a loaf of yeast bread ready for the oven. My husband, the realist, suggested we go immediately to the hospital. In his mind I am sure he had already cancelled Christmas dinner. My mind was fast forwarding to what needed to be done before everyone arrived the next day. I did concede that a trip to the emergency room was required. I just needed to get a few things done first.

I decided the most sensible thing to do right that minute was to take a shower and wash my hair. I reasoned that if they had to put a cast on my wrist, taking a shower was going to be more difficult, if not prohibited. So, that is exactly what I did, with Wart's help, of course. Toleration of my crazy thinking is one of my husband's finest qualities.

Once my hair was dry, Wart put the dog in his carrier and helped me throw a coat around my shoulders. By the time we arrived at the ER, there was no need to ask what brought me there. The hand looked like a rubber glove that had been blown up like a balloon. The hospital staff took x-rays, put on a temporary cast and gave me the name of surgeon to contact. We got home about midnight and I fell into bed exhausted. About two a.m., I was still in pain so I decided to take two pain killers that we had picked up at the all night pharmacy.

I was too tired to read the little labels they put on the side of the prescription bottle. Well, I learned a very valuable lesson that I will not soon repeat. No matter how tired you are, take time to read the fine print. I overlooked the *Take with food* warning and within a half hour, I was so nauseous that I could not get out of bed. I must have dozed off and on, but all I remember was feeling so sick I couldn't drag myself up from the bed.

Christmas morning arrived without any consideration of the night before. Fortunately, my sister, Carol, came to the house early and jumped into action to pull the dinner together. I managed to get out of bed and position myself on the couch. With the aid of an ice pack and pillow, I held the arm in a saluting pose, prepared to answer the "where is this, what's next" questions.

The whole gang arrived and the meal was a success. Everyone laughed, ate and enjoyed themselves. They even pitched in and did all the dishes. I was very happy we had not cancelled.

When I look back, I think of the broken wrist as my early Christmas present. My husband was out of bed and functioning at full speed. That was more important than any box wrapped under the tree.

I wish I could say the treadmill slowed down after Christmas. Little did I know it had an incline mode, too.

Chapter Seventeen

Heavy Hearts

Mom's condition worsened right after Christmas. Another trip to the hospital revealed she had had a stroke. The prognosis was that she probably would not live long enough to be released from the hospital. She did not give up easily. After a few days, they transferred her back to NHC. The family was at her side constantly. She held on, hour by hour, for a month. She was relieved of her pain and suffering on January 23, when God called her home.

The pain endured over the next few months is still too fresh in my heart to share. My words cannot adequately describe the sorrow I felt when each phone call was received. Rather than omit the events from the book, I share the following excerpt from my journal.

Journal Excerpt, March 8, 2010

It is a few hours before the visitation at the Baue Funeral Home. Yes, another funeral. The cards and paperwork are still visible from Mom's funeral and here we are again, gathering to console each other in our grief.

Just forty-six years old, Nancy, Larry's wife, was a vibrant, friendly and loving mother, daughter, sister-in-law, and friend. No one was prepared, least of all her sons who found her lifeless body stretched across her bed in the middle of a sunny afternoon.

There were no words of comfort I could share, just complete silence, when Larry called to tell me. What could I say? With Mom's passing, we were comforted with the knowledge that she was no longer in pain, no longer unable to communicate her aches and fears. She was at peace in a better place.

While I believe there is a better place, it was much too soon for Nancy to be called away. She and Larry had worked so hard to reach this point in their lives. Tommy and Bryan had graduated high school and both were working.

Larry had been reunited with his daughter (from a previous marriage) after years of separation, and he found out he was a grandfather to three of her children. They were ready to take time for themselves, traveling and enjoying life together at another level.

It was determined that Nancy died from an undetected heart ailment. Her absence is a great void in Larry's household and in all of our family gatherings.

Perhaps it was a good thing that the office for which I worked was closing on in July 2011, as an indirect result of the Defense Base Closure and Realignment (BRAC) Commission decision. The hectic pace kept me from giving in to the depression that threatened to bring me down.

Every day, the urgency of transferring all of the work performed in St. Louis to our headquarters in Arlington, Virginia, consumed my thoughts. When not up to my neck in paperwork, I was managing the volatile environment among the employees, planning a closing ceremony, submitting recommendations for special awards and recognitions and disposing of office equipment. I came home exhausted every evening. I didn't have the time to dwell on the emptiness I felt.

In May, our headquarters announced a monetary incentive for early retirement. I made the decision that I would submit my retirement request along with many of the other employees in the office, rather than accept a transfer to Fort Knox, Kentucky, as a liaison for the Agency.

One thing I had learned from life is that it is too short. Foremost in my mind was my desire to have quality time with my husband before either of us met with health issues that would limit our options. The free time would allow me to pursue my love of writing and my poetry and there would be time to volunteer in the community. I knew it was the right decision once I submitted the papers.

On July 30, 2010, I walked out of the building on Page Avenue after thirty-three years and four months as a civil servant. I didn't look back. All the stresses, concerns and frustrations were left behind and I was anxious to start on my new journey in life.

Wart and I renewed our love for fishing. He began taking walks with me, which is something I tried to convince him to do for many years. Sometimes, we'd visit a nearby casino. The choice was ours to sleep in, rise early, or take a nap in the afternoon. Life was good.

The comfort was brief. Another phone call, another tragedy, another painful memory causes the rhythm of my keyboard to pause. Again, I rely on my hand written words from my journal to tell the story.

Journal Excerpt, September 19, 2010

Its midnight and I cannot begin to go to sleep. I keep replaying the phone call from my brother, Rob. Emma fell off the high deck at her home and was airlifted to a hospital in Georgia. She has undergone surgery to remove part of her skull in order to make room for the swelling in her brain. Rob didn't want to bother me, but asked if I have any special connections with God, could I say a prayer for Emma?

Jeff, Rob's youngest son, and his wife, Lisa, flew to Guatemala in January, just a few days before Mom died, to finalize the adoption of Emma and bring her home to Georgia. It was a miracle that the government had finally approved the procedure after delaying the decision more than two years. She turned three years old in July.

I don't feel worthy of asking for a miracle, but I beg God to not only save her life, but to heal her without any trace of injury. I have been struggling with my spiritual health since Mom and Nancy died. I know death is a part of life, but enough. The open sores won't heal when every few months another loved one slips away.

I no longer feel a strong connection to the church and it is hard to talk with anyone about the turmoil I feel inside. I still believe God is with me at all times and my faith has not been shaken, but my foundation has cracks in it.

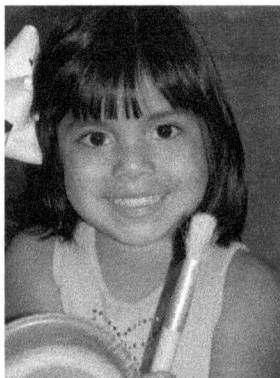

Emma Hootselle

Emma died from her injuries on September 22, 2010..

Chapter Eighteen

Strong Hear

The crisp autumn air is always a welcomed relief after the scorching heat of summer in Missouri. Country drives to view the colorful array of leaves always finds me torn between enjoying the beauty of nature and anticipating the rigors of winter inching closer by the hour.

One beautiful morning in October, Wart drove us to a nearby grocery store. Displays of pumpkins outside the store brought a smile to my face. As soon as we entered the store, we were greeted by rows of candied apples, cider and Halloween treats. We resisted purchasing any of the sweets even though it was tempting.

When we returned to the car, Wart sat in the driver's seat and closed his eyes. When he didn't start the car, I became concerned.

"What's going on?"

"I don't know. Something's wrong. I'm having bad chest pains."

Although Wart had chronic chest pain for years, something was different this time. We traded positions and I made the decision that we were going to the hospital. He began sweating profusely and about a mile from the hospital, he told me he thought he was going to pass out. I pulled over into a parking lot and dialed 911. The dispatcher came on and connected me with a medical person. We were so close to the hospital, yet, if he stopped breathing, how would I be able to help him?

Anxiously I asked "should we wait here for an ambulance or just drive the rest of the way?" I was frustrated with the reply.

"Whatever you think you should do."

This was not the kind of response I anticipated or needed. Wart was shouting "Drive!"

With that, I pulled back onto the road and raced toward the ER. The receptionist contacted the head nurse and they rushed him into a room where they hooked him up to an Electrocardiogram. The nurse tore off the strip of paper from the machine and dashed off.

We had been through similar routines during previous chest pain attacks. In the past, everything was handled at a much slower pace and there was always a delay in receiving the results. This time was different. In less than a minute, the doctor entered the room, along with two of nurses.

"Have you ever had a heart attack?" the doctor inquired.

"No," Wart answered.

"Well, you're having one now." A few minutes later, his eyes rolled up into his head and he quit talking. His heart had stopped and a team of people with a crash cart appeared. There were at least eight medical people surrounding his bed, each performing some function that appeared to be well rehearsed. Someone yelled "Clear." The shock from the paddles lifted his body a foot off the gurney. He came down with a thud. I stood there in shock, unable to breathe.

A few seconds later, Wart picked up the conversation he was having with the doctor as if nothing had happened. The look of surprise on all of our faces made him question what had happened. "Did I pass out or something?"

It was something all right. The doctor looked at me and said, "If he had not been here when that happened, he would be dead." I was glad I had decided to drive him to the hospital, even though the hospital staff had warned me not to do it again in the future.

Within another fifteen minutes, the cardiac team had arrived and so had Laura and Daniel. The nurses began running as they pushed his gurney down the hall to the Cath Lab for surgery. Laura and I could not keep up. My sisters, Carol and Michelle arrived and joined us in the waiting room, anxious for the surgery to be over. It was a Saturday and no one else was in surgery, so when the code blue was announced for the Cath Lab, we knew Wart's heart had stopped again.

The room fell silent. Everyone's eyes were focused on the door, waiting for someone to come through it to give us the bad news.

I could not envision planning his funeral or finding the strength to bury another family member. I was angry and still in shock. No one talked; I could barely hear anyone breathing. Nearly twenty minutes went by before the nurse came out. "He is awake and talking."

I was afraid to trust that his heart would not stop again. Laura and I went into the surgery room and spoke with him and the doctor. He looked good. There were no tubes, no wires, no signs that he had just been brought back to life twice in an hour. He was fortunate to be alive and we knew it.

If it hadn't been for BRAC, I would have been working and things might not have turned out the same. Wart has had two additional stints implanted and is doing well.

It was good to have a happy ending for a change. Yet, it is really the beginning of a new lifestyle. The obligations of my job and caring for my mother consumed much of my day just a short time ago. I struggled with feeling lost for a while. While I have not missed rising before the break of dawn, I missed having goals and accomplishing tasks.

As the days pass, the fractures in my structure have begun to heal. I've learned to find fulfillment in small successes, like finishing this book, because I realize the size of a goal doesn't matter, as long as I have one and work toward it. I continue to move forward, looking ahead just far enough to make sure I'm still on track and glancing back just long enough to see how far I've come. The difficult times in life are what make me strong and remind me to appreciate the times of joy and peace.

A good friend gave me a lovely, leather bound journal when I retired. It was such a beautiful gift, I hesitated to write in it for a long time, afraid I would make a mistake. Then I realized, mistakes are part of life. They are meant to teach us that we are not perfect; never have been; never will be. So, I am beginning to fill the pages with new adventures, and with mixed feelings of excitement and apprehension, as I continue my journey through the **Peaks and Valleys** of the rest of my life.

Diane M. How was born and raised in Pine Lawn, Missouri. She graduated from Normandy Senior High School in 1969 and attended St. Louis and St. Charles Community Colleges and Webster University.

Diane has been an adult volunteer with the Girl Scout Council of Eastern Missouri for more than thirty-five years and has served in many positions, including District Chairperson, Learning Facilitator and Trainer of Trainers. Diane's civil service career, as a supervisor with the Department of the Army, spanned thirty-three years and culminated with her retirement in 2010. During her tenure, she was awarded the Superior Civilian Service Award. Diane's poetry was published in two anthologies and was featured in *The International Who's Who in Poetry,* (2005).